D1596767

SUNDAY HOMILIES
Saint Vincent Archabbey
Cycle B

Demetrius R. Dumm, O.S.B.
Campion P. Gavaler, O.S.B.

ARCHABBEY PUBLICATIONS
2014

Copyright © 2014
ARCHABBEY PUBLICATIONS

300 Fraser Purchase Road,
Latrobe, Pennsylvania 15650-2690
www.stvincentstore.com

All rights reserved. No part of this book may be reproduced or transmitted in any form or by any means, electronic or mechanical, including photocopying, recording, or by any information storage and retrieval system without permission in writing from the publisher.

Scripture texts in this work are taken from Saint Joseph Edition of The New American Bible Revised Edition, © 2010, 1991, 1986, 1970 Confraternity of Christian Doctrine, Inc., Washington D.C. All rights reserved. No part of the New American Bible may be reproduced in any form without permission in writing from the copyright owner.

Library of Congress Cataloging-in-Publication Data

Dumm, Demetrius, 1923-
  Sunday homilies : Saint Vincent Archabbey / Demetrius R. Dumm,
O.S.B., Campion P. Gavaler, O.S.B. -- 1 [edition].
    volumes cm
  Includes bibliographical references and index.
  Contents: -- Cycle B.
  ISBN 978-0-9773909-9-1 (v. 2)
  1. Bible. Gospels--Sermons. 2. Church year sermons. 3. Common
lectionary (1992) 4. Saint Vincent Archabbey (Latrobe, Pa.)--Sermons.
5. Catholic Church--Sermons. I. Gavaler, Campion P. II. Title.
  BS2555.54.D86 2014
  252'.6--dc23
                          2014031583

Printed in the United States of America

Cover photo:
Mosaic of a lion as symbol of Saint Mark the Evangelist in Iglesia de San Manuel y San Benito, Madrid, by architect Fernando Arbos, 19th century. Used with permission.

Archabbey Publications editorial team:
Elizabeth Cousins, Jordan Hainsey, Kimberley Opatka-Metzgar,
Simon Stuchlik and Alexis Zawelensky.
Cover design: Jordan Hainsey.

ADDITIONAL PERMISSIONS

Quote from Fesquest, Henri. *Wit and Wisdom of Good Pope John.* New York: P.J. Kenedy & Sons, © 1964. Print. All rights reserved. On page 73.

Quote from McDonagh, Francis. *Dom Helder Camara: Essential Writings.* ©2009, Orbis Books, NY. All rights reserved. On page 86.

Quote from Hillesum, Etty. *An Interrupted Life: The Diaries, 1941-1943 and Letters from Westerbork.* © Macmillan Publishers, 1996. All rights reserved. On page 90.

Quote from Pope Paul VI, *Nostra Aetate,* #4, 1965. © Libreria Editrice Vaticana, March 31, 2014. On page 136.

Dedicated to
Archabbot Douglas R. Nowicki, O.S.B.

Contents

Ordinary Time 55

Solemnities of the Lord During Ordinary Time

Foreword

Pope Francis has given us a kind of humorous, non-scientific test to discern whether or not the purpose of a Sunday Mass has been realized. Its purpose has been realized if the people leaving church after Mass will look like people who have just heard good news. Perhaps Pope Francis had this simple test in mind when he gave the title "The Joy of the Gospel" to his apostolic exhortation in which he stresses the importance of the homily in announcing good news.

Many priests, religious and lay persons have told me that Father Demetrius and Father Campion in their interpretations of the Sunday gospels have helped them realize that each gospel is, in fact, good news. It is always good news to hear with deeper understanding that the Risen Lord is with us, loving us in all the circumstances of our lives.

It is my hope that the Archabbey's publication of these "Sunday Homilies" by Father Demetrius and Father Campion in book form will help many more people to act, to speak, and to look like people who have heard and who believe the good news of the gospel.

+ Douglas R. Nowicki, O.S.B.

Archabbot Douglas Nowicki, O.S.B.

Advent Season

First Sunday of Advent
Mark 13: 33–37

Gospel Summary

In this gospel passage Jesus illustrates the mystery of his future, final coming in power and glory with a simple parable. He says to his disciples: "Be watchful! Be alert! You do not know when the time will come." He compares his final coming to a man traveling abroad who had placed his servants in charge of his house. The servants must do the work assigned to them, and the gatekeeper must be on constant watch awaiting the return of the master of the house. The parable, with its accompanying admonition to work and watch for the Lord's final advent, completes Chapter 13 of Mark's gospel—Jesus' last teaching before his passion.

Life Implications

The First Sunday of Advent marks the beginning of a new church year: the liturgical actualization for us of the saving events of Christ's life, death, and resurrection. The gospel passage proclaims the essential truth that will be celebrated in all its dimensions throughout the year—namely, the "advent" truth that God has come in the person of Jesus Christ, and that the same Lord, now invisibly present through the Spirit, will come again in power and glory.

This Sunday's homily might serve as an overture, anticipating some of the life implications of the Lord's coming which will be celebrated on the Sundays and holy days of the coming year. Here are a few of the major themes.

In the first reading from the prophet Isaiah, we hear that the exiles have returned from Babylon to find their homeland devastated and the holy temple destroyed. We can remember the prophet's prayerful plea and make it our own at those times when our life-situation appears hopeless, and God seems far away: "Oh, that you would rend the heavens and come down" (Isaiah 63: 19).

Paul, in the second reading from his First Letter to the Corinthians, presents a life implication that can also be a constant throughout the coming year. Paul assures us that the heavens have been rent, and God has come among us. Jesus, the Risen Lord, is now truly "God with us." Because of this grace, we are able to stand firm with the Lord's strength as we await his final revelation in glory. And as we wait, despite difficulties and suffering, we thank God always for the gifts of the Spirit that we have received.

Because the Church gives us the gospel in the context of the celebration of the liturgy, we are reminded that throughout the year the Lord comes, not only to proclaim the word, but also comes to give himself to us as friend and life-giving savior. It is in the context of the liturgy of the Last Supper that Jesus says to his disciples: "I have called you friends" (John 15: 15).

The First Sunday of Advent is also a good moment to hear a major theme of the liturgical drama—every human being, particularly a person in need, is a sign or sacrament of the Lord's coming. In fact, as Jesus tells us in the parable of his final Advent, our treatment of even the least of his brothers or sisters will be the essential criterion of judgment (Matthew 25: 30–46).

Finally, there is the beautiful Advent theme of the sacrament of the present moment. Each moment, each event of our life is a sign of the Lord's coming. Whatever the moment, we can say in faith: It is the Lord. And it is the Lord who awaits our response of love and gratitude.

"The one who gives this testimony says, 'Yes, I am coming soon.' Amen! Come, Lord Jesus!" (Rev 22: 20).

Campion P. Gavaler, O.S.B.

Second Sunday of Advent
Mark 1: 1–8

Gospel Summary

At the very outset, Mark declares his gospel to be the "good news." He dares to say this in a world that is broken and weary because this gospel announces the consistent divine initiative to bring about a new creation where peace and harmony will prevail over pride and violence. This new beginning occurs at the coming of Jesus and easily transcends the original creation in scope and significance. If in fact God's dream for a world of peace and justice has not been fulfilled, it is due entirely to the obstacles which we have placed in its path.

Thus, when Mark tells us that the career of John the Baptist was described already in the words of Isaiah (1: 2–3), he is also telling us that opening the road for the coming of the Lord is still a major problem. The desert is a wild and challenging place, a place that demands attention, for it strips away all that is superfluous in human life. We are still preventing the coming of the Lord by refusing to open ourselves to the radical implications of the message of Jesus.

It is for this reason that the baptism of John is called a baptism of repentance. It represents an expression of regret for having refused to accept fully the implications of the coming of the Lord. On the other hand, it has a positive aspect also which is a declaration of personal readiness to make room in our lives for the Lord, however costly that may be.

Life Implications

One of the major ways in which we prevent the coming of the Lord is our fear that, if we don't focus our attention primarily on our own interests, we will lose control of our lives and be pulled apart by the needs of others. In fact, Jesus means to choose to commit oneself to live as unselfishly as one's freedom permits... which usually means a little more than we think is possible.

This doesn't mean that we should become doormats but it does mean that the needs of others must not be the last and least concern in our lives. In other words, it means to put our lives and our futures into the hands of a gracious God as we strive to make the love and gentleness of Jesus present in our world.

All of this may sound like a life of endless self-denial and very little fun or happiness. However, such a conclusion can be reached only by those who have not really tried to live by the wisdom of Jesus. The fact is that those who really care about others are the happiest people on earth. In this Sunday's gospel, John the Baptist urges us to remove the roadblocks of fear and self-centeredness in our lives and thus assure a truly joyous Advent celebration.

Demetrius R. Dumm, O.S.B.

Third Sunday of Advent
John 1: 6-8, 19-28

Gospel Summary

The gospel passage tells us about a man named John who was sent by God to testify to the light, so that all might believe through him. This is the way the testimony happened. Religious leaders from Jerusalem came to find out who he was. John tells them that he is not the Christ, nor Elijah, nor the Prophet. He does say: "I am the voice of one crying out in the desert, make straight the way of the Lord ... " Then John is asked: "Why then do you baptize ... ?" He answers: "I baptize with water; but there is one among you whom you do not recognize, the one who is coming after me, whose sandal strap I am not worthy to untie."

Life Implications

The life implication of this gospel passage is ultimate in its significance: whether or not we recognize God's coming among us in Jesus Christ. The passage is from the prologue of John's gospel (John 1: 1-34) in which are contained the essential doctrinal truths about Jesus. It is better to read the entire prologue for oneself than to read a summary here. What is essential to note is that in the prologue we have the essential truths about Jesus. Only then does John begin his gospel narrative. Jesus himself now appears on the scene, and personally addresses two men who had heard about him and were following him. Jesus asks: "What are you looking for?" They reply: "where are you staying?" Jesus says to them: "Come, and you will see." (John 1: 38-39)

We, the readers of the gospel, already know from the prologue that Jesus, Son of God and the Word, has dwelt with God and was God "in the beginning." John then in the gospel narrative proceeds to tell us how various people came to recognize the divine reality of Jesus through the gift of faith. Tragically, however, we learn that others, with hardened hearts, failed to recognize him, thus remaining blind in darkness. The gospel tells us about the miracles or signs which occasioned both the recognition and the rejection of Jesus.

At the conclusion of his gospel, John tells us that Jesus did many other signs which he did not write about. But, he adds, these signs are written "that you may [come to] believe that Jesus is the Messiah, the Son of God, and that through this belief you may have life in his name (John 20: 30–31).

The life implication for us is the same as it was for the people who heard about Jesus during his historical life. How do we cross that infinite space between blindness and sight, between hearing about Jesus and recognizing him as the divine person who desires to dwell in us? (Read John, Chapters 14–17.) As in John's gospel, it is through miracles or signs that the divine presence is revealed. For some, John's gospel can become a sign which occasions the recognition of Jesus as living Lord. For others, it may be reading the words of a saint, receiving an act of kindness, seeing a person in need, experiencing an odd coincidence, seeing the beauty of art, music, or nature. Even a tragic event in one's life can become a miracle or sign which leads to the recognition of the divine presence.

Advent is a special time for open-hearted prayer of hope for the gift of recognizing God's coming among us. If today you should hear his voice, harden not your heart. Lord, I believe, help my unbelief.

Campion P. Gavaler, O.S.B.

Fourth Sunday of Advent
Luke 1: 26–38

Gospel Summary

On the carefully programmed Advent journey to Christmas, the Fourth Sunday belongs to Mary. This is so because Christmas, which celebrates the birth of Jesus, necessarily involves the motherhood of Mary. However, the story of that birth is reserved for Midnight Mass, while today's gospel tells us how Mary prepared for that wonderful event by accepting the message of an angel, which meant allowing God to determine how she could be a mother and remain a virgin.

If through the centuries Mary has captured the imagination of the Catholic world, it is in large measure because she faced the mystery of God and said, "Let it be done to me according to your word" (Luke 1: 38). Even her greatest privilege as mother of the Savior presupposes this radical trust and generosity on her part.

It is easy to ignore the mystery of God until the very end of life. It is also easy to live in fear of that mystery. However, human life will never be really successful until we learn to embrace God's mystery with trust and confidence. Mary shows us how to do that and what wonderful results will follow.

Life Implications

Although we know very little about the "historical" Mary, her symbolic presence is real and powerful. In her case, symbolic truth presupposes an historical person but it reveals the universal and perennial significance of that person. It is a truth that transcends such limitations as age, race, and gender as it reveals the meaning of Mary, Virgin and Mother, for all human beings everywhere.

As a virgin, Mary represents hope. Indeed, there are few images that capture the meaning of hope and promise more effectively than that of a youthful young lady. All of us then, who strive to be positive and joyful and hopeful in a weary and despairing society, can look to virginal Mary as a model who is ready and willing to inspire and encourage us.

When considered specifically as the mother of our Savior, Mary is also the most perfect model of fruitfulness. She represents, therefore, both virginal, promising springtime and fruitful, bountiful summer. She conquers cold, barren winter in our hearts and leads us to a rich and meaningful harvest.

There is such a temptation on our part to live off of others and to complain rather than to contribute. Constant complaining and blaming others means an empty harvest. By contrast, Mary models for us a life that is wonderfully fruitful through loving concern for the welfare and happiness of others. There is no better way to prepare for and to celebrate the birth of Jesus!

Demetrius R. Dumm, O.S.B.

Christmas Season

Christmas Season

Christmas
Luke 2: 1–14

Gospel Summary

In the gospel passage for Mass at Midnight we hear the Christmas story from the Gospel of Luke. It is a story so simple that even a child can grasp it; yet, even after 2000 years it is a mystery so profound that the richness of its meaning remains inexhaustible. We are reminded again of God's providential care which makes all history sacred history. The powerful rulers of the world, whether an Egyptian pharaoh or a Roman emperor, may have their armies and issue their decrees, but through the odd coincidences of history, God's own purposes are ultimately achieved. As foretold by the prophet, Mary gives birth to a savior, who is Christ and Lord, in Bethlehem, the city of David.

Caesar Augustus, regarded by the Romans as a god who would bring peace and salvation to the world, is now only the unwitting instrument in the divine plan to bring God's peace and salvation through this child born of a young Jewish woman. Mary is the faithful, willing agent of God's loving care. After giving birth to her son, she wraps him in swaddling clothes and lays him in a manger. Jesus is cared for in the manger of the Lord (Isaiah 1: 3), not in an over-crowded lodging among strangers. Already in the Christmas story, we have an intimation that divine-human love (now as a child in a manger, in a few short years as a young man dying on a cross) offers itself to us in vulnerability. Who can be afraid of such a God? Love cannot force itself, and can suffer the pain of rejection or indifference.

In the gospel passage for Mass at Dawn (Luke 2: 15–20), Luke continues the Christmas story by having shepherds go to Bethlehem and relate the divine message they had received. Mary keeps and reflects upon all these things in her heart. Then the shepherds, like the faithful to this day, join the heavenly, angelic liturgy in glorifying God for all that has happened.

Life Implications

The meaning for us of Luke's Christmas story is completed by the prologue of John's gospel read at Mass During the Day (John 1: 1–18). Christ is born of Mary so that he might be born and live in us. Those who accept the Word who became flesh become the children of God, not by natural generation, but by divine grace. The good news of Christmas will not be fully realized until we can say with Saint Paul: "Yet I live, no longer I, but Christ lives in me" (Galatians 2: 20).

The Church constantly proclaims the truth, which may well be the hope and the challenge of the new millennium: the mystery of the Incarnation sanctifies all human life. The Lord, by accepting a share of our common humanity from his mother, has identified himself with all humanity, even the least of his brothers and sisters (Matthew 25: 31–46). The good news of Christmas will not be fully realized until the dignity of every human being is respected and made secure in terms of the right to live, religious and political freedom, social and economic justice. Mary, in the loving care of her child, becomes the icon of the care that God wants us to extend to every human being, even the most vulnerable. In truth, it is care extended to Christ himself.

In a special way at Christmas we might treasure in our hearts the prayer said by the priest at every Mass in preparation for the Eucharistic Liturgy: "By the mystery of this water and wine may we come to share in the divinity of Christ who humbled himself to share in our humanity."

Campion P. Gavaler, O.S.B.

Feast of the Holy Family
Luke 2: 22–40

Gospel Summary

Today's gospel reading about the presentation of the child Jesus in the temple is most suitable for the feast of the Holy Family because it deals very gently with the difficult question of the relationship of young and old in families and in society generally.

The parents of Jesus are very careful to observe the Jewish laws about offering the first-fruits of family and field to God, thus acknowledging that all blessings come ultimately from a loving creator. This affirms the importance of the Hebrew tradition for the future followers of Jesus. The aged Simeon and Anna are there to represent the people of Israel, who have for so long been yearning and praying for the arrival of the Messiah. They have been living for centuries with scarcely any tangible sign of God's concern for them, but they have not lost hope.

We can well imagine Simeon's joy as God reveals to him that this infant is in fact the long-awaited Savior. For he immediately resigns himself joyfully and trustingly to a future filled with the goodness of God's promises. Anna too sees her patient piety rewarded by this sign of God's response to her persistent prayers.

Life Implications

There are so many of us older people alive today that we need to reflect carefully upon the example offered to us by Simeon and Anna. We do not see in them any sign of resentment as they recognize that their places are being taken by energetic and often impatient younger men and women. They are able to welcome this new and younger world because their prayerful attention to the Lord has established the utter trustworthiness of God's promises of a future life beyond the weakness and the letting go in death.

There are few more remarkable signs of hope than that of older people whose eyes are still bright with the promise of better days in the ultimate future. In fact, the very act of taking an infant into one's arms, as Simeon did, is a profound affirmation of one's sure knowledge that God has given the victory to life.

The effect of this trust in life and in the future is to create an ideal environment for the nurturing of new life. In fact, today's gospel tells us that, when Joseph and Mary welcomed the new world represented by their divine child, "The child grew and became strong, filled with wisdom; and the favor of God was upon him" (Luke 2: 40). All children have the right to be nurtured, day in and day out, with loving attention and trust, so that they too may acquire the freedom and wisdom needed for responsible living.

We must reflect with great sadness on the tragedy of neglected children in our world. They receive so little psychological or spiritual support to enable them to "grow and become strong, filled with wisdom." And we need to be deeply grateful for those parents whose love and care prepare their children for a future that can be both serious and joyful.

Demetrius R. Dumm, O.S.B.

Epiphany
Matthew 2: 1-12

Gospel Summary

The Epiphany gospel is a continuation of the Christmas story in Matthew's prologue to his gospel (Chapters 1–2). The prologue is a theological masterpiece in narrative form through which Matthew anticipates the major historical events he will present in his gospel to explain the significance of Jesus for us.

The names of Jesus are revealed: Messiah, King, Son of David, Son of Abraham, Emmanuel (God with us). As Son of Abraham, Jesus fulfills the divine promise that in Abraham's seed "all the nations of the earth will find blessing" (Genesis 22: 18 and Matthew 28: 10). The miracle of the virginal conception heralds the beginning of the climactic end-time of sacred history. The gentile nations as foretold by the prophet Isaiah come to the New Zion with their treasures to praise the Lord. Jesus will be rejected by many, will suffer persecution and death, but will ultimately triumph through the Father's providential care in the resurrection.

In today's gospel reading, Matthew tells us that when Jesus was born in Bethlehem, magi from the east arrived in Jerusalem looking for the newborn king of the Jews so that they might do him homage. When King Herod heard this, he was troubled, and asked the magi to bring him word of the child's whereabouts so that he too could pay him homage. When the magi found the child with Mary his mother, they did him homage and offered him their gifts. Warned in a dream not to return to Herod, they departed for their own country by another way.

Life Implications

The good news of Epiphany is that Jesus is the revelation of God as one who offers himself to us in love. Jesus is the epiphany of the invisible God in all the events of his life: as a helpless child lying in a manger, as a young man dying on the cross—the ultimate revelation that God's glory is love. This feast reminds us that each Sunday's liturgy with its gospel reading is an epiphany of the Lord to be reflected upon in the quiet of faith.

As in every offering of love, the Lord awaits the response of our heart. Will it be that of Herod who perceives it as a threat to his own autonomy and power? Will it be that of the magi who perceive this offering of love as the fulfillment of the human quest? Epiphany is the revelation of the purpose of the Incarnation: that God and we, God's creatures, might enjoy each other in the embrace of love. Who could be afraid of a God like that?

The church anticipates the good news that the mutual exchange of divine and human love is the deepest meaning of the Incarnation by giving us a reading from the Song of Songs at an Advent Mass a few days before Christmas. This "greatest of songs" is a love poem describing the wonder and excitement of the divine-human exchange of love in beautiful erotic images. The poem can help us realize a bit of the astonishing mystery we celebrate. The Lord says to each of us: "Arise, my friend, my beautiful one, and come" (Song 2: 10). One is also reminded of Christina Rossetti's lovely epiphany poem "In the Bleak Midwinter."

What can I give Him, Poor as I am?
If I were a shepherd, I would bring a lamb;
If I were a Wise Man, I would do my part;
Yet what I can I give Him: Give my heart.

The epiphany of the Lord is actualized in every celebration of the Eucharist. Jesus reveals himself and identifies himself as the bread of life. One could not imagine a more powerful sacrament or symbol to reveal that the ultimate meaning of Jesus is to give himself to us in love. Bread has no meaning by existing for itself. Bread exists in order to give life to those who receive it as food. The prayer after communion for the Mass of Epiphany expresses this mystery of faith: "Help us to recognize Christ in this Eucharist and welcome him with love."

Campion P. Gavaler, O.S.B.

Lenten Season

First Sunday of Lent
Mark 1: 12–15

Gospel Summary

The Spirit drives Jesus into the wilderness where he is tempted by Satan. We should recall that this event in Mark's gospel comes immediately after Jesus' baptism in the Jordan. As the heavens are torn open, the Spirit descends upon him, and a voice comes from heaven: "You are my beloved Son" (Mark 1: 11). After the stark, matter-of-fact statement that Jesus was tempted by Satan, Mark tells us that after John's arrest, Jesus begins his mission: "The kingdom of God is at hand. Repent, and believe in the gospel." (Mark 1: 15)

Matthew and Luke in their narratives of the temptations include Jesus' triumph over Satan in a dramatic verbal exchange between them. Mark does not present the temptations in this way because his entire gospel is a narrative of the trials that Jesus undergoes. Satan tempts him to doubt that he is God's beloved Son, and likewise tempts him to betray his mission on behalf of God's kingdom. Satan will use every means to tempt Jesus in order to save his own kingdom that has dominance in the world.

Jesus is tempted by his own disciples. "Get behind me, Satan. You are thinking not as God does, but as human beings do," Jesus said to Peter (Mark 8: 33). He is tested frequently by enemies from among his own people and by the Romans. His own relatives say that he is out of his mind (Mark 3: 21). The most severe temptation comes when he appears to have failed in his mission; he is misunderstood, betrayed, and abandoned by his disciples; he is arrested, undergoes the humiliation and torture associated with a criminal's public execution; and finally he apparently has the experience of being forsaken by God while dying on a cross. Yet, his dying prayer in this dark night of the soul is also a cry of unconquered hope and trust (Mark 15: 34, Psalm 22).

The Letter to the Hebrews reveals the good news that the triumph of Jesus over the most severe temptations imaginable can be a source of hope and trust in the trials that we undergo. "For we do not have a high priest who is unable to sympathize with our weaknesses, but one who has similarly been tested in every way, yet without sin" (Mark 4: 15). "Because he himself was tested through what he suffered, he is able to help those who are being tested" (Mark 2: 18).

Life Implications

No one with the consciousness of freedom escapes the testing that reveals where the heart's true treasure lies. Only the incidentals of the testing differ for each of us. The heroes of faith down to the present day triumph over their trials because they share the single-minded, childlike faith of Jesus. Jesus in his human consciousness and freedom loved God with all his heart, and with all his soul, and with all his strength (Deuteronomy 6: 5). A person with a divided heart, on the other hand, easily fails in a test of faith, and particularly in a trial of suffering constantly asks God, Why? Further, the double-minded person demands some evidence of God's presence and care.

The life-implication of Mark's gospel is that we must pray as Jesus prayed if we hope to love God as he did with an undivided heart when our time of trial is upon us. Like Jesus before his great trial in the garden of Gethsemane, we may pray that if possible the hour of trial might pass by us. Nevertheless, with the power of his Spirit we must also pray: "Abba, Father, all things are possible to you. Take this cup away from me, but not what I will but what you will" (Mark 14: 36). Jesus then said to Peter, "Simon, are you asleep" (Mark 14: 37)? Shortly after Jesus was arrested. Peter, standing among the crowd, was tested by the high priest's maid. Unprepared by prayer and fearful for his life, with a curse Peter denied that he even knew Jesus.

At the Eucharist for the first Sunday of Lent a good prayer would be to ask the Spirit to heal the illusions, desires, and the doubts that divide our hearts. Only with this grace can we say the Lord's prayer with all our heart, and with all our soul, and with all our strength. And with Christ's Spirit we can live without fear because we trust that God's will for us can only be love.

Campion P. Gavaler, O.S.B.

Second Sunday of Lent
Mark 9: 2–10

Gospel Summary

Today's gospel brings us a story about the illumination of Jesus on a mountaintop in the presence of his closest disciples, Peter, James, and John. Tradition tells us that this mountaintop was Mount Tabor. However, the name of the mountain is not given in any account of the Transfiguration and so we are invited to ponder the symbolic significance of this major event in the ministry of Jesus.

The illumination of Jesus has traditionally been interpreted as a light from heaven to show divine approval of his mission after he has just announced to his disciples that "the Son of Man must suffer greatly" (Mark 8: 31). This creates a problem, however, because only three of the disciples are present and future developments do not show that they were reassured. It is far more likely that the light is coming from within Jesus as his face glows in a full awareness of the surprising nature of the mission that his heavenly Father has assigned to him.

Jesus certainly must have wondered about a mission that would result in his becoming a political Messiah, bringing violence and war, as his disciples and the crowds expected. Now he sees clearly that his mission of salvation is through loving and ultimately dying for others. His illumination, therefore, would be an ecstatic moment of discovery. And that is why Moses and Elijah join him there, for they too have experienced God's revelation on a mountaintop!

In this moment of mystical experience, Jesus also hears a voice from heaven, which repeats the words heard at baptism but then adds, "Listen to him" (Mark 9: 7). This suggests that he is now prepared to share the ultimate wisdom of God, namely, that loving and sacrificing are the only way to conquer sin and death ... and thus to enter into resurrection glory.

Life Implications

There is something very comforting about the fact that Jesus experienced a kind of mystical illumination that was followed by his direct movement to Jerusalem and the climax of his mission as our Savior. For this reminds us that we too need to reexamine the basic orientation of our lives and to ask whether we are willing to adopt the wisdom of Jesus which counsels us to put aside the dominant quest for satisfaction and security in this life and to accept a new way of living that is marked by a desire to be of service to others.

When we realize that the words "Listen to him" are directed to each one of us, we must take very seriously the implications of such a command from God. This surely must mean that we too are expected to "visit" this mountain of the Transfiguration, where we can be "illuminated" by the sure knowledge that, when all is said and done, the most important thing that we can do in this life is to "die," as Jesus did, because we love and care for others.

We may think that this means nothing but self-denial, but the fact is that those who seek the happiness of others more than their own satisfaction turn out to be the happiest people of all. This doesn't mean becoming a doormat or catering to obsessive dependants, but it does mean that we are sensitive to others and truly committed to their welfare. This daily "dying" leads to ultimate resurrection life. It is also an excellent way to keep the spirit of Lent.

Demetrius R. Dumm, O.S.B.

Third Sunday of Lent
John 2: 13–25

Gospel Summary

Since the Passover was near, Jesus goes up to Jerusalem to celebrate the festival with his fellow Jews. When he arrives at the temple area, he drives out those who were selling animals for sacrifice as well as the money changers, saying, "Take these out of here, and stop making my Father's house a marketplace." When the temple authorities (the "Jews") demanded a sign from Jesus for what he had done, he said, "Destroy this temple and in three days I will raise it up." After Jesus was raised from the dead his disciples remembered what he had said. They realized he was speaking of the temple of his body, and came to believe the Scripture and what he had spoken. John adds that Jesus was able to recognize true belief in him because he could read the human heart.

Life Implications

The idea of where one lives or dwells is perhaps the central theme of the fourth gospel. John begins his gospel by telling us that Jesus is the Word who became flesh and made his dwelling among us. "In the beginning" the Word was dwelling with God, and the Word was God. Immediately after his baptism in the Jordan, we hear the first words that Jesus speaks in the fourth gospel. He sees two disciples of John the Baptist following him and says to them, "What are you looking for?" They reply. "Rabbi, where are you staying?" Jesus replies, "Come, and you will see." (John 1: 38–39)

We already are alerted to the fact that John's gospel is a gospel of incarnation. Its essence is sacramental or symbolic: the extraordinary is actualized in the ordinary. The eternal Word becomes present and is revealed by dwelling among us. Thus we realize that the disciples' question about where Jesus is dwelling is not merely about a street address somewhere in Galilee. When Jesus replies "Come, and you will see," we realize he also means seeing with the eyes of faith. When he speaks to his disciples, we realize he is also speaking to us.

The astonishing good news that Jesus reveals is that anyone who believes in him will dwell where he dwells, with the Father. John's gospel is the narrative of the signs that Jesus does so that those whom he encountered then, and those who hear the gospel now might believe and have life in him (John 20: 31). John presents various types of people who refuse to see the extraordinary through the signs, and also the beloved disciples who do see and come to believe in Jesus.

Today's gospel is a prophetic warning so that we will not be like the temple authorities who do not see that Jesus is the one sent by God to dwell among us in new ways. Jesus' action in the temple is in the tradition of the prophets. They rebuked the people who thought they were safe by coming to the temple while committing all sorts of abominations (Jeremiah 7). Jesus, like the prophets before him, loved the temple, but he is warning us that even the most holy created realities can become obstacles to believing in him and believing what he has spoken. The temple truly was the dwelling place of the divine presence: the holy place of prayer and communion with God. The temple authorities believed this, but they had narrowed their vision, and thus were unable to see that Jesus himself was the new temple. He himself is the indestructible dwelling place of the divine presence, of prayer and communion with God.

We can reduce the meaning of the Christian sacraments to suit our own purposes, and thus close our eyes to other signs of the divine presence to which the sacraments point. For Catholics the most holy sacrament of the Risen Lord's presence is the Bread of the Eucharist. It is possible to believe in this sacramental divine presence and at the same time to ignore what Jesus has spoken to us of his presence in the least of his brothers and sisters. It might give us pause to note that the criterion of final judgement that Jesus tells us about is not whether we recognize his presence in the Eucharist, but whether we respond with compassion to his presence in the least of his brothers and sisters (Matthew 25: 31–46).

Campion P. Gavaler, O.S.B.

Fourth Sunday of Lent
John 3: 14–21

Gospel Summary

In today's gospel selection, Jesus continues his discussion with Nicodemus on the subject of baptism. It is important to note this because there is no explicit mention of baptism in this passage. This does not mean that the author has somehow lost his train of thought. What it does mean is that, though the water ritual of baptism is important, what really matters is the quality of faith on the part of the one who is being baptized.

Jesus gives us the wonderful good news that "... God so loved the world that he gave his only Son." We are included in that world, and it should be most comforting to hear that we are loved by the One who is most capable of loving. But we must also notice that the liberating effect of that divine love will be available to us only to the degree that we believe. "Whoever believes in him will not be condemned, but whoever does not believe has already been condemned." It is of the greatest importance, therefore, that we understand what this believing means in our daily lives.

Life Implications

It is tempting to think that believing in Christ means simply that we affirm the creed, or that we agree that Jesus existed and worked miracles and died and rose from the dead. To accept these truths is important but this is not what is meant by "believing" in this passage. In fact, one can sincerely affirm all these facts theoretically and still live very selfishly. To believe in the One who was "lifted up" means nothing less than to make his self-offering part of our own lives through daily concern for others; it means to live unselfishly. This is the only kind of faith that will give us eternal life.

Most of us were baptized as infants with no conscious awareness of what was happening. Our sponsors promised, in our names, that we renounced Satan and affirmed Christ. It was hoped that our sponsors and others will explain all that to us when we became old enough to understand the very serious commitment made for us. Unfortunately, we usually expect our sponsors to do little more than to remember our birthdays ... and often less than that.

The simple fact is that those baptized as infants must "claim" their own baptisms, as it were, as soon as they are old enough to do so, which usually means in early adulthood. The sacrament of baptism is not magic, and its graces become fully operative in our lives only to the extent that we accept and live the promises made years ago in our names.

When we promise to renounce Satan, we are declaring our firm resolution to eliminate from our lives the "big lie" of Satan, namely, that we can achieve happiness by thinking only of ourselves. And when we commit ourselves to Christ, we firmly resolve to follow his example of unselfish, thoughtful concern for others. When we are thus "lifted up" like Jesus on the cross of love, we can be sure that we will also be "raised up" with him in the victory of resurrection. Some may think that this takes all the fun out of life, but in reality the people who love in this way are the only truly happy people in the world. But we won't know that until we try it!

Demetrius R. Dumm, O.S.B.

Fifth Sunday of Lent
John 12: 20–33

Gospel Summary

Some Greeks who had come to Jerusalem for the Passover feast say to Philip, "Sir, we would like to see Jesus." Jesus responds, "The hour has come for the Son of Man to be glorified." He then says that in order to produce much fruit, a grain of wheat must fall to the ground and die; and only the person who "hates his life in this world will preserve it for eternal life." Those who follow him, Jesus promises, will be where he is, and the Father will honor them.

Jesus, realizing that his "hour" will involve suffering and death, is troubled; yet, he entrusts his life to the Father. Through giving himself to his Father's will, the world will be judged, and the ruler of this world will be driven out. Jesus then reveals the purpose of the "hour" he is about to enter: "And when I am lifted up from the earth, I will draw everyone to myself."

Life Implications

The incident of the Greeks asking to see Jesus marks a turning point in the fourth gospel. Before, as at the wedding feast at Cana, Jesus had always said that his "hour" had not yet come. Now through the symbolic presence of the Greeks, Jesus will be able to draw everyone to himself—Gentiles as well as Jews, people today as well as people of the first century. We, too, would like to see Jesus.

One of the most elusive concepts in the entire bible is "glory." John uses the term to refer to the divine presence manifesting itself in the world, and also to the recognition of that supreme presence by a faithful person. In the hour that has come upon him, how will the Father's presence manifest itself to Jesus, and how will he honor that divine presence? It is clear from many incidents in the fourth gospel that Jesus loved and enjoyed his human life. He took part in a wedding feast at Cana. At the death of his friend Lazarus, Jesus was moved with the deepest emotions (anger or indignation as well as sorrow). He wept, so much did he love his friend. Now that his "hour" has come, Jesus is troubled at the prospect of losing his life. The Letter to the Hebrews states: "In the days when he was in the flesh, he offered prayers and supplications with loud cries and tears to the one who was able to save him from death...." (Hebrews 5: 7).

Because human life is so precious, perhaps the deepest human instinct is for its survival. We seek power and possessions to secure it. We seek pleasures to enjoy it. We seek honors to assure ourselves of its worth. Jesus, too, faced the temptation to make the preservation of his own life his supreme value. In prayer, however, he recognized the presence of the Father's eternal life dwelling in him, and he committed himself to his Father's will even if it meant he would die. In this the Father glorifies his name by showing us in Jesus that divine life and love overcome death, not only in his beloved Son but in every human being who follows Jesus.

When Jesus dies on the cross, it appears to be the "hour" when the "ruler of this world" has triumphed once and for all. However, the reality is that Jesus is lifted up not to end his life on the cross, but is lifted up to eternal life in the Father. The good news that John's gospel proclaims is that now Jesus draws everyone to himself. The Greeks and all who now "see" Jesus and follow him in faith will be where he is, with God.

The crucial "hour" when one must choose either to love one's life in this world above everything else, or to love one's life in God, of course, will come in the particular circumstances of one's own world. There are immediate implications of that decision. To define one's ultimate meaning in relation to any reality but God is to live in a state of anxiety because that finite reality, however precious, may pass away at any moment. On the other hand, to define one's meaning in relation to life in God brings peace beyond understanding. Even though, like Christ, we may experience the deepest emotions at the death of a loved one, or be troubled at the prospect of our own death, the final word is peace. "I have told you this so that you might have peace in me. In the world you will have trouble, but take courage, I have conquered the world" (John 16: 33).

Campion P. Gavaler, O.S.B.

Passion Sunday
Mark 14: 1–15: 47

Gospel Summary

For us Christians, the story of the Passion, Death, and Resurrection of Jesus represents the climax, not just of the earthly career of our Lord, but of all biblical revelation. The first part of this Passion story, without the Resurrection, is the gospel selection for this last Sunday of Lent.

It is impossible to comment on all the elements of this lengthy and incredibly rich gospel passage, and so I have decided to offer some thoughts on a little "story-within-the-story," which is the anointing of Jesus by an unnamed woman at the very beginning of the narrative. At first glance, this episode appears to be completely irrelevant and we may be tempted to dismiss it until we read, at the end of the story, that it is indispensable to the Passion story itself: "... wherever the gospel is proclaimed to the whole world, what she has done will be told in memory of her."

This story is so important because it is related to the Passion of Jesus in the same way that a key signature is related to the music that follows. What this woman did, therefore, tells us how to read and understand the Passion of Jesus. Briefly stated, her seemingly extravagant anointing of Jesus represents, in microcosm, what Jesus himself is about to do for the whole world. Just as she breaks open the exquisite alabaster cruet and pours its precious and fragrant ointment on the head of Jesus in anticipation of his death and burial, so also Jesus will allow his body to be broken in death and will pour the precious ointment of his life-blood on all of us who are destined to die.

Her action is considered wasteful and foolish by the bystanders, so that Jesus must correct them as he praises this woman for her generosity. And, in like manner, what Jesus does may appear to be foolish and wasteful to an unbelieving and cynical world, but his Father will raise him from the dead and thereby confirm forever the wisdom of his generosity.

Life Implications

If we take this little story of the anointing of Jesus seriously, we will learn that the passion story is not primarily about how much Jesus suffered, but rather about how much he loved. He did suffer, of course, and his suffering was intense. But suffering as such is not necessarily redemptive. What makes the pain and suffering of Jesus the source of salvation for us is the fact that it resulted from his extraordinary loving. We all know that suffering can come from other sources than loving, such as not getting our own way or being wedded to false goals, but this kind of selfish suffering has nothing in common with the suffering of Jesus.

And so, for example, when we make the Way of the Cross (the Stations), we may be tempted to say: "I'm with you, Jesus. I'm suffering just as you did!" But Jesus could very well say to us, "Are you suffering because you love? If so, by all means join me, and we will walk together toward Resurrection. Otherwise, please try to learn the real meaning of love." The love of Jesus is unselfish and therefore will always involve the pain of self-denial. In like manner, good parents suffer as they make sacrifices for their children, just as children suffer when they try to be more mature and unselfish. Some suffering always results when we place the needs of others before our own interests. Old people also suffer when they trust God's goodness and promises in spite of the apparent hopelessness of their situation. But it is also true that such loving sacrifice always brings with it real joy, as well as the promise of eternal happiness.

In this very real human suffering that inevitably follows real loving, we can be comforted by the assurance that we are being anointed with the precious blood of Jesus. This enables us to walk with him on the way of the cross—that loving, painful path that leads to glory. When we do this, we too will be called foolish and be told that we are wasting our lives by not working for ourselves alone. But Jesus will tell us, as he told that generous and sensitive woman, that what we do is not foolish but "a good thing." Nothing can be more comforting than to hear Jesus make such a wonderful judgment about our feeble efforts to walk with Jesus.

Demetrius R. Dumm, O.S.B.

Easter Season

Easter Sunday

John 20: 1–9

Gospel Summary

John's gospel ends as it began, with the question: where does Jesus dwell? Immediately after his baptism by John the Baptist in the Jordan, Jesus noticed two of the Baptist's disciples following him. He said to them, "What are you looking for?" They replied, "Rabbi, where are you staying?" Jesus said to them, "Come, and you will see" (John 1: 38–39). Now at the end after his death and burial, Mary of Magdala goes to the tomb while it is still dark to visit this final earthly dwelling place of Jesus. Seeing that the tomb is empty, she finds Simon Peter and the disciple whom Jesus loved, and says to them, "They have taken the Lord from the tomb, and we don't know where they put him."

Peter and the other disciple run to the tomb. Peter enters the tomb first and sees the burial cloths there, and the "cloth that had covered the head, not with the burial cloths but rolled up in a separate place." The other disciple follows Peter into the tomb; he sees and believes. John adds that they did not yet understand the Scriptures that Jesus had to rise from the dead.

Life Implications

The climax of the Easter gospel and the essence of its implications for us lie in the statement "he saw and believed." Coming to believe in the Risen Lord is the purpose and the point of the entire gospel: "Now Jesus did many other signs in the presence of [his] disciples that are not written in this book. But these are written that you may [come to] believe that Jesus is the Messiah, the Son of God, and that through this belief you may have life in his name" (John 20: 30–31). John wants us to identify with the two disciples of John the Baptist who ask Jesus, "Where are you staying?" He also wants us to identify with the "beloved disciple" who runs to see where Jesus is so that we, like him, will see and come to believe. The end of John's gospel begins our encounter with the Risen Lord.

The "sign" that leads the beloved disciple to believe is the cloth that had covered the head of Jesus. John is the only evangelist who mentions this cloth so we know it is significant in his narrative. The disciple upon seeing it very likely connects its meaning with the head cloth that Moses put aside when he ascended to speak face to face with God (Exodus 34: 33–35). Now the beloved disciple realizes with an intuitive leap of faith that Jesus, one greater than Moses, has ascended to be face to face with God in glory. Jesus no longer dwells in a tomb; he is alive and has gone to dwell with the Father as he had promised. In the following episodes John then relates how the community of disciples comes to believe that Jesus has also kept his promise to return to be with them through the Spirit (John 14: 3–18). It is now possible through faith to dwell where Jesus dwells, in God.

Was the head cloth that the beloved disciple saw proof that Jesus rose from the dead and had ascended to the Father in glory? Of course not. However, for him it was a sign like the other signs of the gospel that could lead to belief. A sign that leads to faith or to a deeper faith in the Risen Lord is unique for each of us: the head cloth led the beloved disciple to believe, but not Peter. For one of us, it may be hearing the gospel or homily on Easter Sunday. For another it may be the experience of seeing a spring flower or listening to Mahler's "Resurrection Symphony." What is needed on our part is unconditional commitment and openness in seeking truth: "Whoever lives the truth comes to the light..." (John 3: 21).

Each of us is called to believe and to become a beloved disciple. Each of us is called to dwell where Jesus dwells and to have life in his name. For this gift of God's love we are grateful, and in this faith we can celebrate Easter with hope and joy.

Campion P. Gavaler, O.S.B.

Second Sunday of Easter
John 20: 19–31

Gospel Summary

The first thing that we notice in today's gospel is the amazing effect that the presence and words of Jesus have on his confused and frightened disciples. He finds them in hiding, completely immobilized by the terrible realization of the death of their beloved leader. He addresses them cheerfully with the standard greeting: "Peace." Under normal circumstances, this simply means that one wishes another well. But it means far more than that when spoken by the risen Lord. The disciples feel that the world is out of control. Jesus assures them that such is not the case. In fact, he is there to offer them the gift of deep and unshakable confidence. In spite of dire appearances, all is well.

The reason that all is well is because Jesus now offers them the Spirit. This Holy Spirit has the ability to enter the deepest recesses of their being and to make Jesus more truly present to them than he ever was when they knew him in the flesh. Jesus offers the same Spirit to us also and this Spirit can make Jesus wonderfully present to us. For it is this same Spirit who convinces us of the love of God for us … and, to the extent that we know that, we have nothing to fear.

We recall how God took his good spirit from King Saul and gave it to King David (1 Samuel 16: 13–14). The consequence was dramatic. Saul would slip deeper and deeper into darkness and despair, while David seemed to lead a charmed life in spite of sins and tragedies. In fact, he became the model of the Messiah and has been a favorite subject for sculptors and painters ever since.

Thomas was not there to receive the Spirit and so he could not trust the good news that the other disciples shared with him. However, when he met Jesus later, everything changed and he allowed Jesus to become thenceforth the center of his life. The witness of others is always important, but nothing can replace a personal encounter with the Lord.

Life Implications

One need not look far in our world today for attitudes of cynicism and distrust. We should avoid becoming gullible or naïve, of course, but we must at all cost learn how to trust. The risen Lord offers us his Spirit and, if we open our hearts to that best of all gifts, we will be able to trust when it is proper to do so.

Most of all, we will trust God's promises, which tell us, in essence, that we can share in the life of Jesus if we dare to be kind and thoughtful and loving in a world that is too often thoughtless and cruel. We really cannot be trusting without the help of God, but with that help we can avoid the terrible pessimism of Saul and acquire the positive, hopeful spirit of David. This positive spirit is found everywhere in the Psalms, which have been attributed to David, not because he wrote more than a few of them, but because the authors of these beautiful prayers were all people like David.

A special gift of the Spirit is the confidence and freedom that allows us to forgive others. Life is just too short for holding grudges or for nursing old injuries. And when we let go of these burdens we will enter more and more into the joy and generosity of the Spirit. In this way, we will not only be free to face the future with courage but we will also become much more pleasant fellow travelers for those who are making the journey with us.

Demetrius R. Dumm, O.S.B.

Third Sunday of Easter
Luke 24: 35-48

Gospel Summary

On that first Easter Sunday of the Lord's Resurrection, two disciples return to Jerusalem from their journey to Emmaus and recount to their friends how Jesus was made known to them in the breaking of bread. Suddenly, Jesus appears in their midst and says, "Peace be with you." They are terrified and think they are seeing a ghost. Jesus says to them, "Why are you troubled? And why do questions arise in your hearts?" He then asks them to look at him and to touch him. After assuring them that he is the same person they knew before his crucifixion, he eats some baked fish with them.

Jesus then explains how the Scriptures reveal that the Messiah would suffer and rise from the dead; and that repentance for the forgiveness of sins would be preached in his name to all nations, beginning in Jerusalem. He then adds, "You are witnesses of these things."

Luke concludes his gospel with this Easter Sunday appearance of Jesus to his disciples as the threshold to its climax and also to its meaning for us. After telling his disciples that they are "witnesses of these things," Jesus declares: "And behold I am sending the promise of my Father upon you; but stay in the city until you are clothed with power from on high." The first reading of this Sunday's Mass from the Acts of the Apostles (also written by Luke) tells us the good news that Jesus kept his promise by sending his Spirit, the promise of his Father. The age of the Church has begun: Peter with the power of the Spirit and in the name of Jesus proclaims those things the disciples had witnessed.

Life Implications

Luke first wants to assure us that though faith in the Risen Lord is a divine gift and a decision of acceptance beyond reason, nevertheless its basis is the solid ground of reason. The Christ of faith is not the creation of the disciples; he is the one they knew during his earthly life. The same words that are used to describe everyday realities are used to describe the reality of Jesus. Yet, here as in other New Testament appearance accounts, it is clear that the new, transformed reality is not subject to the laws of chemistry or physics. This is to assure us that Jesus does not possess a body revived from the dead. He exists in a divine mode of existence; he is able to appear suddenly, no longer bound by the laws of space, time, and matter.

Luke's gospel together with his Acts of the Apostles may well be called the good news of the Holy Spirit. Its background is the bad news that all humanity is in a state of alienation from God and alienation within itself. The divine action of merciful forgiveness and reconciliation began with the presence of the Spirit guiding the chosen people, Israel (Acts 28: 25). It is the same Spirit who from beginning to end enabled Jesus to advance the divine plan to its next stage. "Jesus returned to Galilee in the power of the Spirit... The Spirit of the Lord is upon me..." (Luke 4: 4–21).

Now in the final climactic appearance to his disciples, the Risen Lord authorizes them to begin the end stage in fulfillment of the divine plan. It is the age of the Spirit's action in the Church whereby Christ's mission to preach repentance and forgiveness of sins is extended to all nations. Jesus knew that without his Spirit the disciples and those who would follow them would be totally incapable of fulfilling his mandate.

Each Sunday we listen to readings from Scripture in order to learn how the Spirit was with Jesus, and how the Spirit wishes to inspire us. Thus, in the first reading of this Sunday's Mass from Acts, we see a new Peter speaking through the power of the Spirit. Now he and the other disciples are no longer paralyzed by fear. They speak, often in hostile situations, with the confident, joyful candor and boldness of Christ himself. (This is the "parrhesia" of Acts 2: 29; 4: 13, 29, 31; 28: 31.) It is the Spirit who enables us to know Christ and to live as he lived. In the second reading,

John tells us we can be sure that our knowledge of Christ is true faith if we keep his commandments—essentially to love others as he has loved us.

The Spirit also enables us to share in the Easter joy of Christ. The complete joy of the Spirit's presence is anticipated in the disciples' experience of the Risen Lord: "They did him homage and then returned to Jerusalem with great joy" (Luke 24: 52). Today in our breaking of bread with the Lord, we pray for the grace to accept the gift of the Spirit, the promise of his Father, with all our heart so that we might live and act as Christians without fear—in freedom, in truth, in love, in joy.

Campion P. Gavaler, O.S.B.

Fourth Sunday of Easter
John 10: 11–18

Gospel Summary

In our largely urban society we tend to glamorize sheep herding. In fact, and especially in Jesus' day, it was a lonely, harsh, and dangerous occupation. Jesus was not using hyperbole, therefore, when he says that the good shepherd must be ready to lay down his life for the sheep. It is only the bad shepherd, for whom the sheep are of merely utilitarian value, who flees because he is unwilling to risk his own life when they are attacked.

Jesus is not really talking about sheep herding, of course. He is speaking instead about the intimate, personal bond that must exist between him and his followers. He offers his life for them, and they respond in total trust, so that they know and love Jesus in the same deeply personal way that Jesus knows and loves his heavenly Father.

Life Implications

We live in a world that seems to prize personal freedom above everything else. The problem with that is that one person's use of freedom may easily infringe upon the rights of someone else. In such cases, one must recognize that, in a society of many individuals, personal freedom cannot be absolute. When Frank Sinatra sang, "I did it my way," he was making beautiful music but expressing very dubious theology. The ideal is to live life, not in my way, but in the right way.

When Jesus says that he is the good shepherd, he certainly means that he sacrifices his comfort and safety for the sake of others. There is a graphic description of bad shepherds in Ezekiel (Ezekiel 34: 2–3): "Woe to the shepherds of Israel who have been pasturing themselves! Should not shepherds pasture the flock? You consumed milk, wore wool, and slaughtered fatlings, but the flock you did not pasture." Such selfish shepherds do not care for their sheep at all but instead mistreat them as they use them for the satisfaction of their own needs.

If we wish to be followers of the good shepherd, we must have that same relationship with God that Jesus did. This means that we must open ourselves to the reality of God's love for us and then do all that we can to make that love a reality in the lives of others. This will often mean that we will place the interests and needs of others before our own wishes and preferences. In other words, we will often "do it their way." This may, at first glance, appear to be a recipe for disappointment and servitude, but such a conclusion will be reached only by those who have never tried it. The good shepherd is also a happy shepherd!

This concern for others will create in us that wonderful sense of "knowing" Jesus and being "known" by him. In other words, we will sense the presence of Jesus in our lives in a way that transcends all the external elements of religion. These elements will remain important but we will understand that they are really meant to lead us to a personal and mystical experience of Jesus in all the circumstances of our lives. When that happens, we will recognize instinctively the voice of our good shepherd and gladly follow him into God's wonderfully mysterious future.

Demetrius R. Dumm, O.S.B.

Fifth Sunday of Easter
John 15: 1–8

Gospel Summary

In this passage from the Last Supper Discourse (John 13: 31–17: 26), Jesus reveals to his disciples and to us that he is the true vine planted and cared for by his Father. We are the branches, depending on Jesus for life just as branches depend on the vine. "Whoever remains in me and I in him will bear much fruit, because without me you can do nothing." Separated from Jesus we cannot bear fruit: like a useless branch we are cut off and soon wither.

To be certain that we have some sense of how radical the gift of sharing his life is, Jesus adds two astonishing statements. If we ask for anything, our Father will give it to us because of the communion of life. It is as though his own beloved Jesus were asking. "Father, I thank you for hearing me. I know that you always hear me," Jesus prayed before restoring his friend Lazarus to life (John 11: 41–42). Further, if we bear much fruit from the new Christian life that we have been given, the Father will be glorified in us as he was through Jesus.

Life Implications

At our Eucharist today we hear the gospel as the Christians of John's community at the end of the first century heard it, not with the incomplete knowledge of the disciples before Jesus' death, resurrection, and the coming of the Holy Spirit. We have heard the complete good news beginning with the response of Jesus to the question two disciples asked, "Rabbi, where are you staying? He said to them, 'Come, and you will see'" (John 1: 38–39).

Throughout the Last Supper Discourse, Jesus reveals that he dwells in the Father and the Father dwells in him. And he reveals further that he dwells in us and we dwell in him like a vine and its branches. John's placement of the "vine and branches" saying in the context of the Last Supper reminds us of what Jesus said after feeding a large crowd with bread and fish: "Whoever eats my flesh and drinks my blood remains in me and I in him. Just as the living Father sent me and I have life because of the Father, so also the one who feeds on me will have life because of me" (John 6: 56–57).

If we had only the image of the vine and branches, we might draw the conclusion that our finite human life is totally absorbed by infinite divine life. Rather, the good news is that the communion of life in Christ is a communion of love. "As the Father loves me, so I also love you. Remain in my love" (John 15: 9). Life in Christ is a gift freely given, and a gift freely accepted. Tragically, because there is freedom, the life and love of Christ can be rejected.

The fearful possibility of separation from Christ is a consequence of freedom. It is the possibility of seeking an illusory life that the world separated from God offers. The archetypal figure of the disciple Judas, who succumbed to greed in betraying Jesus, is a graphic reminder of that possibility for all of us. We are meant to live in the peace and joy of the Easter gospel, however, not in fear and uncertainty.

"Without me you can do nothing," Jesus tells us. But with him we can do anything. If we remain in his life and love, we can ask anything of the Father and it will be given. Mindful that Jesus out of love for us, and that his Father might thereby be glorified, he did not ask to be saved from his hour of suffering (John 12: 27). We too will always ask to live in his truth and love. In confident hope that the supreme grace of remaining in Jesus will always be given, we can keep his commandment to love each other as he loved us. Thus, the Father's goodness will also be revealed in us for his honor and glory. "And the way we know that he [Jesus] remains in us is from the Spirit that he gave us" (second reading, 1 John 3: 24). In this knowledge of faith and hope is our peace and joy.

Campion P. Gavaler, O.S.B.

Sixth Sunday of Easter
John 15: 9–17

Gospel Summary

This gospel passage is filled with beautiful statements about the ever-popular subject of love. Jesus tells us that the Father loves him, and that he in turn loves us, and that we should love one another. Perhaps we have heard these sentiments expressed so often that we no longer realize how profound and dramatic they really are.

When Jesus says that the Father has loved him, he is correcting a very common concept of God. Many people at that time (and perhaps ever since) pictured God as someone very transcendent and therefore very distant from them. He was surely all-powerful but, like most powerful ones, he seemed to be cruel as well. Is God not in some way responsible for famine and natural disasters? Does he not at least permit the death of young parents and innocent children?

But Jesus tells us that he knows God much better than we do. As eternal Word, he dwells in the lap of his heavenly Father (John 1: 18). This is body language, which tells us that Jesus hears the very heartbeat of his Father. He assures us that God is a loving Father who wishes only good for us. Most of all, he knows that this loving Father offers us a love that can enliven and nurture and energize us, just as the sun energizes plants and trees.

Jesus invites us to experience and to trust this life-giving love, to live in the presence of it, and to yearn for it, just as the sunflower follows the sun across the sky in our human gardens. Then we will know how to become sunshine in the lives of others. We will also know how to deal with mysteries in our lives. We will also want to share our treasures with others and thus become part of that divine love that overcomes all darkness and evil.

Life Implications

The implications of this vision of reality are not hard to see. Most people who do not love, or do not love enough, are usually persons who do not feel that they themselves are loved. It is futile to tell people that they must love others when they have not really been made free to love by experiencing love in their own lives. Too often it is a case of impoverished people trying desperately to give more than they have.

That is why it is so important to hear and to trust the words of Jesus about the love of the Father for us. This love is found in Jesus himself, who gave his life for us, but it is also found everywhere in life: in loving family and friends, in the blessings and successes of life, in every flower and gentle breeze.

Today's gospel challenges us to acknowledge the dark evil in life but it asks us to notice especially the luminous good that is also there. And as we pay attention to the good in life, we will be able to let the evil go by or, at least, to keep it in its place, which is never at the center of life. This is exactly what Jesus did and, with him, we too need to feel the warmth of the Father's love and to share that warmth with all whom we meet in life.

Demetrius R. Dumm, O.S.B.

Seventh Sunday of Easter
John 17: 11b-19

Gospel Summary

This passage is part of the high-priestly prayer of Jesus that John uses as the climax of the Last Supper Discourse. Its beauty of poetic expression and depth of meaning cannot be captured in a prosaic summary. A summary at most serves as a focus for study in preparation for hearing the prayer in its proper context of the Eucharistic liturgy.

Jesus prays that those who believe in him may be one just as he is one with God, his Holy Father. In his prayer Jesus says that he came into a hostile world to save those the Father gave him from destruction by the evil one. Jesus now is coming to the Father. He will consecrate himself for his disciples so that they may also be consecrated in truth. He will send them into the world as the Father sent him into the world.

Life Implications

A key for grasping the life implications of Jesus' prayer lies in the final verse: "And I consecrate myself for them, so that they also may be consecrated in truth." To consecrate himself means that Jesus offers himself as sacrifice to God, his Holy Father. The word sacrifice, like consecrate or sanctify, refers to the realm of God, the Sacred or the Holy One. In opposition to the realm of the Holy in John's gospel is the "world," hostile to God because it is under the dominion of the "evil one." We who are of the world cannot by our own efforts cross the infinite divide into the realm of the Holy. It is only God who invites and enables us to come into the sanctifying presence through offering ourselves as sacrifice. The offering of self is not complete without God's acceptance. Only then are we consecrated through the gift of being touched by the Holy.

An essential consequence of giving oneself to God is that one belongs to God, and thereby exists for God's use. Otherwise, sacrifice would be as meaningless as giving someone a car, while retaining its use for one's own projects. The gift of consecration by God through sacrifice always involves a mission to advance God's projects in the world.

Of the great variety of sacrifices in the biblical tradition, one is particularly significant in regard to Jesus' high-priestly prayer at the Last Supper. In this tradition a person could offer an animal representing oneself to God. The animal is burned to signify passage into the realm of the Holy. God accepts those making the sacrifice, and invites them to share a sacrificial banquet as an expression of divine communion that has been given. The experience of communion with God is the reason that offering sacrifice of whatever kind in the biblical tradition is associated with joy.

Deuteronomy 16: 11–12 illustrates the life implications of offering oneself in sacrifice: "You shall rejoice in the presence of the Lord, your God, together with your son and daughter ... as well as the resident alien, the orphan, and the widow among you, in the place which the Lord, your God, will choose as the dwelling place of his name. Remember that you too were slaves in Egypt." We see the joy of celebrating a sacrificial banquet with God. And we see that God uses the one consecrated by the divine presence to serve the destitute and the outcasts of society. If you give yourself to God in sacrifice, you will be used for love.

In his high-priestly prayer Jesus says: "But now I am coming to you ... And I consecrate myself for them." (John 17: 13, 19) Jesus' entire life was a coming to God as sacrifice. Jesus did not offer an animal representing himself; he gave himself in his entire humanity. The climactic completion of his sacrifice comes when he is lifted up on the cross and is accepted by the Holy Father in the resurrection.

At the Last Supper before the completion of his sacrifice, Jesus reveals the good news that his disciples will be consecrated as he is consecrated. With the same mission as was given to Jesus, they will be sent to bring the fallen world, which God loves, into the joy of divine life. In the Catholic tradition, Christ's presence in the mystery of his eternal sacrifice is actualized in every celebration of the Lord's Supper. Today, we also hear the good news that our self-giving becomes one with the self-giving of Jesus. In the joy of this undreamed of communion with the sacrifice of Christ, we offer our prayer of thanks and praise. We share the sacrificial banquet to which God invites us, receiving Jesus himself as food and drink for eternal life. Then the Lord sends us into the world as he was sent to become bread and wine for others, so that all may rejoice in being one with him in the life and love of God.

Campion P. Gavaler, O.S.B.

Ascension of the Lord
Mark 16: 15–20

Gospel Summary

In the last chapter of Mark's gospel, we hear the Risen Lord issuing to us a solemn challenge: "Go into the whole world and proclaim the gospel to every creature." This is not so much a call for proselytizing as it is a reminder that we should want to share the wonderful gift of faith with which we have been endowed. If we realize how important this wisdom of Jesus is for ourselves, we will never tire of offering it to others.

The mysterious signs that will accompany those who believe are surely to be interpreted symbolically. The ability to cast out demons, or to speak in new languages, or to be immune to poison, or to heal the sick represent the spiritual effects of a living and dynamic faith. The positive and hopeful witness of the believer will overcome the negative and destructive influence of those forces that represent the dark and chaotic powers that constantly attempt to destroy the harmony and goodness of God's creation.

Life Implications

When we recognize this symbolic interpretation of the effects of living faith in our lives, we discover that vibrant faith has the power to enable us to make the spiritual journey through life successfully. In biblical times, dangerous serpents often lay along the path of those traveling on foot. Drinking from unfamiliar wells could also lead to a fatal illness, such as a new strain of typhoid to which one had not become immune. On the spiritual journey of faith, these would represent the two most dangerous challenges to face us, namely, cynicism and despair. Our journey to God is especially threatened by a negative and destructive spirit, which contradicts the wisdom of unselfish love and makes fun of those who would live by such wisdom.

The reference to healing hands in the present text refers to the comforting and healing presence of believers who offer the ill a witness of hope that transcends all our fears of sickness and mortality. Sometimes the laying on of hands can bring recovery, but this passage refers more likely to a spiritual presence that gives ultimate encouragement to those who are fearful about the uncertainty that their illness brings to their lives. When we offer to the ill a sense of God's presence and love, we also give them an assurance that no threat in this life can withstand the power of God's goodness.

The ability to deal successfully with all these problems in our fragile lives comes, therefore, from the power of a loving God who can never forget or abandon us. We are told that Jesus was "taken up into heaven," but we also hear that "the Lord worked with them and confirmed the word (of the gospel) through accompanying signs." The clear implication is that the Risen Lord, now seated at the right hand of God, is prepared to help us now more than he ever did in the days of his earthly existence. For this reason we should sing constantly, even if it is at times "in the rain."

Demetrius R. Dumm, O.S.B.

Pentecost Sunday
John 20: 19–23

Gospel Summary

On Pentecost Sunday we celebrate the wonderful good news that the risen Lord has poured out his Spirit upon us, first of all to convince us of his victory over sin and death, and then to enable us to continue his work of salvation by our own love and concern for others.

As we can well imagine, the disciples were filled with fear and foreboding after the death of their master. But suddenly Jesus is there among them radiant with life. He shows them his terrible wounds, which have now become beautiful emblems of his love for them. He offers them his peace—that deep, calm, resonant sense of confidence, which is so different from the peace that the world can offer—a superficial peace that amounts to little more than a temporary cessation of hostilities. This profound peace becomes possible through the presence of his Spirit in them.

And then Jesus tells them what possessing the Spirit will mean in their lives. Henceforth, they will need to be converted from their natural tendency to be self-centered to an attitude of loving concern for others. And this will be manifested first and foremost by their willingness to forgive others. This would be impossible if we did not enjoy the powerful presence of the Spirit who enables us to overcome our constant judgmental tendencies.

Life Implication

As fragile human beings, we know the experience of living in fear and of being anxious and worried about many things, some of which exist only in our imagination. Jesus, having absorbed the ultimate violence, offers us his peace and thereby enables us to be confident and joyful in the face of even severe uncertainty and threat. This represents a real experience of liberation from the paralysis of fear—a paralysis that often prevents us from doing beautiful and risky things, like giving cut flowers!

With this peace and joy comes the obligation to share our blessings with others. It was once thought that the command of Jesus to forgive or retain sins was addressed only to priests and referred only to the Sacrament of Reconciliation. Now it is clear that this charge is addressed to all the followers of Jesus. We must all accept the wonderful and awesome responsibility of offering or withholding forgiveness. In this case, the sin of omission looms large and should make us all examine our consciences in regard to the many times that we may have persisted in nursing old injuries or have refused to make allowance for extenuating circumstances in the lives of those we call sinners.

In this regard, we should recall the very strong words of Jesus in the Sermon on the Mount: "Stop judging, that you may not be judged. For as you judge, so will you be judged, and the measure with which you measure will be measured out to you." (Matthew 7: 1–2) When we face the final judgment, we all hope to have a merciful judge and now we know how to assure that happy outcome.

It is, of course, very difficult to achieve such an ideal of forgiveness. And that is why Jesus offers us the Holy Spirit who, if given half a chance, will empower us to become the kind of gentle, caring, and compassionate persons that can make a real difference in a world that desperately needs the witness of love and forgiveness. Let us all rejoice in this wonderful gift of the Spirit.

Demetrius R. Dumm, O.S.B.

Ordinary Time

Second Sunday in Ordinary Time
John 1: 35–42

Gospel Summary

John the Baptist, standing with two of his disciples, upon seeing Jesus exclaims, "Behold, the Lamb of God." When Jesus notices that John's disciples are following him, he says to them, "What are you looking for?" They reply, "Rabbi, where are you staying?" Jesus responds, "Come, and you will see." Andrew, one of the disciples, goes to find his brother Simon, tells him they have found the Messiah, and introduces his brother to Jesus. Jesus looks at him and says, "You are Simon the son of John; you will be called Cephas (which is translated Peter)."

Life Implications

There is a true story about a professor who was invited to give a lecture at a major conference on religion. The subject of his lecture was the nature of God. His many hours of research were rewarded by the enthusiastic response he received upon completion of the lecture. On the flight back to his university, however, his euphoric satisfaction about his work was shattered when it dawned on him, as he later reported: "I talked to everyone about God, but God."

We can easily have an experience similar to that of the professor as he was preparing his lecture about God. With a little research we can discover many interesting, even beautiful things about Jesus and his disciples.

Thus, in today's gospel passage, we discover that when the two disciples ask Jesus where he is staying or dwelling the question isn't simply about a street address. John uses the same Greek verb (translated as "staying or dwelling") when Jesus at the Last Supper tells his disciples that he "dwells" in the Father and the Father "dwells" in him (John 14: 10–11). We also discover that when Jesus says "Come, and you will see," the essential meaning of "seeing" is the seeing of faith (John 9). Only with that seeing can the disciples know where Jesus truly dwells, with-in the Father.

Thus far there is no life-implication for us beyond appreciation of a narrative about Jesus and his disciples. A life-changing implication occurs only when we realize that Jesus is addressing each of us today in as personal a way as he addressed the two disciples. The gospel is essentially about an encounter with the Risen Lord now, not about historical knowledge, however orthodox, about Jesus. The historical-critical method of scholarship (like John the Baptist) can give us valuable information about Jesus, but this knowledge cannot enable us to see Jesus in faith—that seeing is a gift of the Spirit.

Because faith means a personal union of friendship with Christ through his Spirit, life implications will be unique and particular for each person. Nevertheless, from the life of Christ and the lives of the saints, certain patterns emerge that are actualized in the particularity of each person's life. Union with the Risen Lord means to share his relationship with the Father. It means that each of us is able to hear with Christ "You are my beloved" and to say with Christ "Thy will be done."

To be in communion with Christ means to pray, always and everywhere. The second reading of today's Mass (1 Corinthians 7: 32–35) shows us that a disciple's personal union with Christ through his Spirit is the foundation of choices about moral behavior. Finally, we see that through union with Christ the saints are not defeated by the setbacks of life. Saint Paul speaks for them all when he wrote: "What will separate us from the love of Christ? Will anguish, or distress, or persecution, or famine, or nakedness, or peril, or the sword? No, in all these things we conquer overwhelmingly through him who loved us" (Romans 8: 35–37).

Campion P. Gavaler, O.S.B.

Third Sunday in Ordinary Time
Mark 1: 14–20

Gospel Summary

Today's gospel tells us that Jesus went to Galilee to begin his messianic ministry. We have become so accustomed to hearing this that we no longer notice how odd it was. Jerusalem was the religious and political center of Israel and anyone announcing a new future for Israel would have been expected to declare his intentions there. As Jesus' ministry develops, however, it becomes clear that Jerusalem was the one place in Israel that was least likely to accept his message. The powerful people in the capital city had far too much to protect. They could tolerate only a "controlled" reform.

Mark wastes no time in pointing out the implications of the public mission of Jesus in Galilee: "This is the time of fulfillment." All the hopes and dreams of Israel are about to be realized. The thousand-plus years of waiting are over. This is so because "The kingdom of God is at hand." The hopes of Israel had been centered in the promised messianic kingdom through which God would deliver his people from bondage and bring everlasting peace. At long last the promise is being fulfilled; the Messiah has arrived.

But the kingdom that Jesus had in mind was both far less and far more that anyone in Israel had imagined—far less, because it would not mean the end of the hated Roman occupation; far more, because it would reveal a Messiah who is the Son of God. Thus, as their small dreams were crushed, unimaginable divine dreams were being substituted. To nurture these dreams, Jesus would choose, not clever politicians, but simple honest fishermen. He knew that for his purposes a good and generous heart was more important than a proud and ambitious head.

Life Implications

This gospel seems especially appropriate for the early years of a new millennium, for we are painfully aware that, though 2000 years have passed, we have not yet seen the fulfillment of God's promises. The solution to this dilemma is the recognition that the fulfillment envisioned by Jesus is constantly being offered to us. It is a "rolling" fulfillment that each person must discover in his or her own lifetime. As such, it should be the primary project of our lives. Jesus has come, but he is also still coming, and each one of us must ask whether he is being welcomed. Fulfillment is offered; it is never imposed.

To live in the expectation of fulfillment is to live in the bittersweet world of promise. What we hope for is still awaited, and that is painful; but we also live in joyful expectation of what will be, and that is comforting beyond words. We may be struggling in a dark valley, but the horizon is illuminated by God's utterly trustworthy promise.

We note that Jesus called his first disciples from their workplaces. This is a reminder that there is a purpose in life beyond work and that this larger purpose is found in our response to God's call to walk with him. This means taking time for prayer and gradually getting to know the Lord as the very center of our lives. For we must come to understand that it is in him alone that the value of our work and the precious gift of other people will be found again and again...unto eternity.

Demetrius R. Dumm, O.S.B.

Fourth Sunday in Ordinary Time
Mark 1: 21–28

Gospel Summary

Jesus goes to the synagogue in Capernaum with four of his disciples where people are astonished that he teaches with such authority. A man in the synagogue, possessed by an evil spirit, recognizes Jesus as the "Holy One of God" who has come to destroy the spirits of evil. After Jesus casts out the evil spirit, the people in the synagogue are amazed at the power and authority that Jesus possesses, and go out to spread his fame throughout Galilee.

Life Implications

More of the implications of this passage may reveal themselves if we remember the narrative context into which Mark places it. After this cure of the demoniac, Jesus cures Simon's mother-in-law and many others afflicted either by illness or by evil spirits.

It is with these acts of power done out of compassion for the needs of others that Jesus begins his public life. Immediately before, Mark has told us of the baptism of Jesus, with the Spirit descending upon him and the voice from heaven saying to him, "You are my beloved Son." (Mark 1: 11) Jesus is then tempted by Satan not to trust that affirmation. After the arrest of John the Baptist, Jesus goes to Galilee where he proclaims that the kingdom of God is at hand. He calls disciples to follow him, and together they go to the synagogue at Capernaum (today's gospel passage).

The cure of the demoniac represents the beginning of the messianic age when the power of Satan's kingdom will at last be destroyed ("Have you come to destroy us?"). Jesus enters a world in which Satan reigns, teaches with the authority of God, and with compassion casts out evil spirits that hold people in bondage and fear. Christ's mission, begun here, will not be completed until the end, "when he hands over the kingdom to his God and Father, when he has destroyed every sovereignty and every authority and power … The last enemy to be destroyed is death" (1 Corinthians 15: 24–26).

Jesus called disciples to be with him as he began his mission at Capernaum; now he calls us to be with him as he continues his mission in the towns and cities where we live. The Spirit descends upon each of us at baptism, and a voice from heaven says to each of us, "You are my beloved." We, like Christ, will often be tempted by Satan not to believe these words when the power of evil seems to be invincible. We will also be tempted to use power and authority, not with Christ's compassion in service of others, but to advance our own reign.

Later in his gospel, Mark talks about authentic Christian discipleship. Two disciples who were with Jesus at Capernaum (James and John) seem to have assumed that discipleship means enjoying positions of power. Jesus summoned all his disciples and explained his notion of power. He said that among the Gentiles, rulers make their authority felt and lord it over people. But, he added, among his disciples, whoever wishes to be great must be the servant of all. This was the notion of power that led Jesus to teach, to cast out demons, to cure illnesses, and finally to give himself up to death on a cross with the supreme power of love. "For the Son of Man did not come to be served but to serve and to give his life as a ransom for many" (Mark 10: 45).

Campion P. Gavaler, O.S.B.

Fifth Sunday in Ordinary Time
Mark 1: 29–39

Gospel Summary

In Mark's gospel, Jesus is presented as one who acts rather than as one who speaks. The lengthy discourses in Matthew, for example, are missing in Mark. This is in keeping with the biblical conviction that actions speak louder than words. It is the interventions of God in human history, at the Exodus of Israel and then in the definitive Exodus of the Resurrection of Jesus, that contain the essential source of biblical revelation. This reminds us also that we must personally participate in some way in those events of liberation in order to receive the salvation promised by the Bible.

In today's gospel, Mark draws our attention particularly to those who were possessed by demons. Whatever their malady may have been, it represented the sad condition that existed before God brought a light-filled, harmonious world out of the original darkness and chaos. Jesus continues this creative work and the demons, as contemporary agents of the old chaos, instinctively recognize him as their adversary.

It is poignant to see how Jesus is already beginning to disappoint his disciples. They cannot wait for him to raise the flag of rebellion and to use his power to drive out the Roman occupiers of their land. But he goes off instead to a quiet place to commune with his heavenly Father. He has come to preach the good news of salvation through the power of love and sacrifice, rather than through the military power and domination that they seek.

Life Implications

We need not look far to find the reality of chaos and dissention in our world today. The ancient Hebrews saw in the original chaos an aggressive force that was constantly trying to take back the creation that God had brought forth. Their imagery may have been primitive, but their perception was very accurate. In fact, the forces of chaos seem at times to have the upper hand today, as nations are consumed by ethnic hatred, communities are divided by strife and families are often torn apart by sibling rivalries. Sometimes the chaos enters our own psyches as we struggle to see the meaning in our lives.

God is fully aware of these troubles and he has sent Jesus to give us the wisdom, which alone can bring us peace and happiness. This is the unlikely, but only truly valid, wisdom of loving concern. Jesus not only taught this wisdom but he lived it fully as he gave his life for us.

We, like the disciples, are all for making war to achieve our purposes, but Jesus goes away to pray. This does not mean that we should not strive to achieve legitimate objectives but it does mean that, ultimately, it is only prayerful attention to the Lord and sincere love of others that will heal the beautiful world that God has entrusted to us and bring the peace and harmony that Jesus came to offer us. For God certainly wishes, once again, to look at our world and be able to recognize, as he did at the beginning, that It is "very good" (Genesis 1: 31).

Demetrius R. Dumm, O.S.B.

Sixth Sunday in Ordinary Time
Mark 1: 40–45

Gospel Summary

This passage continues the narrative of Jesus' mission immediately following his baptism in the Jordan and the call of the first disciples. As beloved Son and Messiah, his mission is to proclaim the good news of the coming of God's kingdom. God's rule over all creation would bring to an end the domination of Satan, characterized by all forms of untruth, violence, sickness, and death. That the power of God's rule is present in Jesus becomes evident to the amazement of the people by his teaching with authority, his healing, and his casting out demons.

This Sunday's gospel tells us of Jesus' cure of a man afflicted with leprosy (a term referring to any repulsive skin disease). A leper comes to Jesus and begs to be cured. Moved with compassion, Jesus touches the "untouchable" and cures him. He then sends him to a priest so that he can be reinstated into the community.

After curing the leper, Jesus had admonished him not to publicize what had happened. Mark here anticipates a major theme he will develop more explicitly in his gospel: namely, that people, even Peter and the rest of his disciples, will misunderstand Jesus' mission. The theme reflects an aspect of Satan's attempt to entice Jesus to redefine his mission solely to the satisfaction of people's temporal needs, and thereby to become the messiah of his own earthly, political kingdom. The kingdom of Satan would remain essentially intact had Jesus succumbed to that temptation. John's gospel also alludes to Jesus' concern about the mistaken notion people had of his mission: "Since Jesus knew that they were going to come and carry him off to make him king, he withdrew again to the mountain alone … you are looking for me not because you saw signs but because you ate the loaves and were filled" (John 6: 15–26).

Jesus, however, is faithful to his Father's will to the end. Filled with divine compassion, he responds to the temporal needs of people for healing and for food; but ultimately he wants to give the gift of eternal life with God, the only gift that will satisfy the restlessness and the hunger of the human heart.

Life Implications

Since the Church is the means by which Christ extends his mission for the sake of God's kingdom through history, healing will be an essential characteristic of its service. Christians, through the urging of Christ's compassion, must bring healing to the world's sickness, making possible medical care even for the "untouchables" of our own society. In the Catholic tradition, Christ's compassionate hand touches the sick in a special way through the sacrament of anointing. The Church like Christ will be tempted to reduce the meaning of God's kingdom to the relief of people's obvious and pressing temporal needs. Christ's compassion, however, continues to extend beyond these needs to the deepest human need for personal transformation through communion in eternal, divine life. We can see how Christ's compassionate hand touches the sick in both aspects in the prayers appointed for the administration of the sacrament of anointing.

Like Jesus each of us will endure a trial of faith when beset by suffering and approaching death. Am I really God's beloved daughter? Am I really God's beloved son? Is it death that defines the meaning of human existence? The source of our hope is that we share Christ's own unconquerable hope through the gift of his Spirit. Jesus prayed to be delivered from suffering and death; nevertheless, as things worked out, he trusted in God's love through the experience of his suffering, abandonment, and dying. In our time of trial, as the Letter to the Hebrews tells, we must keep our eyes fixed on Jesus, the leader and perfecter of faith. "For the sake of the joy that lay before him he endured the cross, despising its shame, and has taken his seat at the right hand of the throne of God" (Hebrews 12: 2).

Campion P. Gavaler, O.S.B.

Seventh Sunday in Ordinary Time
Mark 2: 1–12

Gospel Summary

This Sunday's gospel passage recounts the story of Jesus' cure of a paralytic. We must not be distracted by the ingenious efforts of the paralytic's friends to lower him through the roof because they could not get through the crowd. After all, this story is about salvation, not engineering!

Jesus seems to have sought out paralytics because his miracles are so often for their benefit. This makes good sense when we realize that the miracles of Jesus were intended to show that he came to liberate and therefore people with "frozen" muscles were prime candidates for illustrating this.

The story also makes it clear that the real liberation brought by Jesus is spiritual and eternal, which is revealed when Jesus declares that the paralytic's sins are forgiven. This is the only liberation that we absolutely must have. Cure of a physical ailment is most desirable but it is only a temporary relief.

The scribes are shocked and scandalized to hear Jesus proclaim forgiveness of sins. Instead of rejoicing to hear that this wonderful power is now available, they choose to cling to their own narrow interpretation of religion. Human knowledge alone is ultimately pessimistic.

Life Implications

We are all in so many ways victims of paralysis in the sense that we find it very difficult to realize our potential. Low self-esteem, expressed usually in our fear of trying something new or of making a mistake, not only denies others the benefit of our gifts but also contributes to our own unhappiness. The only solution to this dilemma is our willingness to trust the goodness that God has put in our lives—a goodness that is revealed to us by the gift of faith.

This gift of faith is intended to do far more than merely help us accept the words of the creed. Its real purpose is to enable us to trust the goodness that comes to us from God, but also from loving persons and from the beauty of God's creation. Thus, faith enables us to see the often hidden goodness in life—a goodness that is sometimes hard to discern but which is always available to those who are looking for it. The effect of this experience of goodness is to liberate us and thus to enable us to let go of the evil and hurt that are also a part of every life.

This power of faith in our lives is not something that we can discover by simply wishing for it. Like the paralytic in this story, we too need to count on friends who are usually more than willing to help us to meet Jesus and to hear those precious words: "Your sins are forgiven," and, "Rise, pick up your mat and walk." When this happens, we will gladly join others in declaring, "We have never seen anything like this."

Demetrius R. Dumm, O.S.B.

Eighth Sunday in Ordinary Time
Mark 2: 18–22

Gospel Summary

People come to Jesus and ask why his disciples do not fast, while the disciples of John and the disciples of the Pharisees do fast. Jesus responds: "Can the wedding guests fast while the bridegroom is with them... But the days will come when the bridegroom is taken away from them, and then they will fast on that day." Jesus comments that no one uses a new, unshrunken piece of cloth to repair an old coat, or pours new wine into old wineskins. If one does, the coat will be ruined; or the new wine will burst the old wineskins.

Life Implications

The first reading from the prophet Hosea provides the key for entering the profound mystery that Jesus alludes to in today's gospel. In the passage from Hosea, the Lord says that he will be husband to his people Israel: "I will betroth you to me forever ... with justice and with judgment ... with fidelity, and you will know the Lord" (Mark 2: 21–22). Portraying God as the husband in a marriage-covenant with his bride, the people Israel, is an astonishing image which runs like a golden thread throughout the Old Testament (Hosea, Jeremiah, Isaiah, Ezekiel, Song of Songs) and continues in the New.

By the time of Jesus, the expectation was that the complete realization of the marriage-covenant with God would come with the final age. In his response to the question about fasting, Jesus proclaims that the long-awaited messianic age had arrived. Jesus is the bridegroom who brings the promised future reality into the present. Even though the present reality of Roman occupation, death, and mourning seems to be the only reality, something new has come into being—not from the human past, but from God's future. The new reality is a marriage feast, a time for celebration not a time for fasting.

Jesus lives in the circumstances of his historical life in the radical new way that will characterize life in the future marriage feast of God's kingdom. The Book of Revelation gives us sense of what that future reality is like. There will be a new heaven and a new earth; God will dwell with his people; he will wipe away every tear from their eyes, and there shall be no more death or mourning; there will be rejoicing because the wedding day of the lamb has come (Revelation 19: 7 and 21: 1–4). In a word, the future reality that Jesus makes present now is God's reign through a communion of love.

We can readily understand that for Jesus to live in that future reality as already present must have been disconcerting if not threatening to his contemporaries. Many of his radical teachings, such as the seemingly impossible command to love one's enemies or to live without fear, make sense only in that light. For Jesus even death, which can penetrate every aspect of life through fear, had lost its power to be the final word about his human existence.

The good news is that Jesus invites us to share his faith so that like him we can recognize and live the reality of the future kingdom now, in the circumstances of our own lives. It is a crucial moment of decision: the future is now—or never. The Letter to the Hebrews alludes to the power of faith to bring the reality of the future into the present: "Faith is the realization of what is hoped for and the evidence of things not seen" (Hebrews 11: 1).

Christ the bridegroom has been taken away in regard to his presence in a particular time and place in history. Mark and the hearers of his gospel were well aware, however, that the bridegroom is present in a new way through the Spirit beyond the limits of a particular time and place. Christ says to us now, particularly at his wedding-banquet of the Eucharist: "I will betroth you to me forever ... with justice and with judgment ... with fidelity, and you will know the Lord." "Let us rejoice and be glad... For the wedding day of the Lamb has come, his bride has made herself ready" (Revelation 19: 7).

Campion P. Gavaler, O.S.B.

Ninth Sunday in Ordinary Time
Mark 2: 23–3: 6

Gospel Summary

Whether we read this Sunday's gospel in the longer or shorter version, it still comes down to a dispute about the meaning of Sabbath observance. The Pharisees had a very strict interpretation in this regard and Jesus challenges their attitudes. To appreciate what is at issue here, we need to recall the origin of the Pharisees. They emerged as an identifiable movement in Israel during the previous centuries when God seemed to have abandoned Israel. Their land was occupied by foreigners and there was no prophet to guide or console them.

In this tragic situation, some Jews directed their attention more and more to the Mosaic Law at hand, rather than to God, who seemed to have become hopelessly distant. This resulted in an intense devotion to study of the Law and the development of a body of detailed and meticulous applications of the Law to human circumstances. The sad result for many was virtual worship of the written Law and a consequent neglect of the supreme law of love. For legal observance must always be tempered by the compassion and forgiveness required by an attitude of love and mercy.

In this way, the Pharisees are a perfect example of a pious, and in some ways admirable, devotion to law and order which is essentially misguided. They achieved a kind of personal satisfaction from their rigid observance but made the fatal mistake of neglecting the more difficult observance of the supreme law of love.

Jesus was "grieved at their hardness of heart" (Mark 3: 5), for hardness of heart means being self-righteous and judgmental. Even scrupulous legal observance is of little value under such circumstances.

Life Implications

When Jesus challenges the strict legal observance of the Pharisees, he is not at all suggesting that laws are unimportant or that license can be condoned. But he does make clear that laws are guidelines for good living and must not become an end in themselves. As such, they must be constantly monitored to ensure that they are in fact in service of the ultimate law of love. Laws without love and compassion soon become oppressive and tyrannical.

There is always a grave temptation to replace love, compassion, and forgiveness with mere legal observance. Such strict observance provides one with a sense of virtue and superiority while allowing ample room for pride and self-righteousness. Saint Paul had this in mind when he insisted that salvation comes through grace rather than good works. He goes on to point out, however, that those who live in grace will inevitably produce good works also and without the danger of corrupting pride.

Some people in the Church today are much too quick to judge others and to think that their way is the only way. They often badger Church authorities, urging them to condemn those whose views they do not share. This is indeed a perilous attitude. The Church is for everyone and must make room for many points of view, except of course when ultimate truth is at stake, which is far less often than some would like to believe. After all, the ultimate success of salvation is a vibrant and tolerant diversity, not a boring uniformity.

Demetrius R. Dumm, O.S.B.

Eleventh Sunday in Ordinary Time

Mark 4: 26–34

Gospel Summary

Jesus teaches the meaning of the reign or kingdom of God by way of two parables. In the first comparison, the reign of God is like seeds that a man plants in the soil. It is not the man, however, but the soil that makes the seeds sprout and grow in a way the man does not understand. In the second comparison, the reign of God is like the smallest of all seeds. Yet, once it has completed its growth, it is so large that birds can build nests in its shade. Mark mentions that Jesus further explained the meaning of parables to his disciples.

Life Implications

An immediate life implication is present in the means that Jesus uses to help us understand the meaning of God's reign—that is, through parables. He uses images from our common experience whose truth is evident in order to give us some insight into a reality whose truth is not evident. A parable is a literary form that better fits the category of non-fiction, rather than fiction: it is not simply an imaginative story. Jesus uses parables to make us aware that we are a living part of a deeper, real story. Some response on the hearer's part is thus inescapable—whether it be to ignore, to reject, or to accept the truth of the parable as pointing to the ultimate meaning of one's life. Jesus had explained to his disciples that some people may hear a parable, "but worldly anxiety, the lure of riches, and the craving for other things intrude and choke the word, and it bears no fruit" (Mark 4: 19).

In the two parables of today's Gospel, Jesus gives us an insight into the mystery of God's reign. We have already learned that the purpose of Jesus' ministry is to preach the good news of the reign of God (Mark 1: 14). The good news is that God has not abandoned his human family, fallen and wounded, living in bondage under the reign of satanic powers (Mark 3: 20–30). It is the will of God to liberate and to reunite the human family through a divine reign of parental love, which ultimately will prevail over satanic violence and deceit. We see the meaning and the complete realization of the reign of God's love in the life, death, and resurrection of Jesus of Nazareth. And in the Church that Jesus founded, we see the beginning of the complete realization of God's reign in the entire human family.

Because the reign of God is a reign of love, it is not realized unless the divine self-giving to us is accepted and lived in human freedom. The Lord's Prayer beautifully expresses the decision to accept and to live in God's reign. It is the necessary context of all the parables.

Jesus in the two seed-parables addresses the human tendency to believe that human fulfillment comes mostly through our plans and efforts. As a result, when things do not turn out as we have planned and worked to achieve, we become discouraged and lose hope. Jesus reminds us that the coming and growth of God's reign is the work of God's love. Its complete realization will be evident only when the Son of Man comes in glory. Our response to this truth about the reign of God is to pray for its coming on earth as it is in heaven. Further, it is to do our utmost to prepare for its coming in the particular circumstances of our lives.

The story is told that upon his election Pope John XXIII was unable to sleep because the seemingly insurmountable problems facing the Church were pressing upon him. Then the personal meaning of the seed-parables dawned on him. He was able to pray: "Listen, Lord, this Church is yours not mine. I'm going to sleep." Only in this trust was John XXIII liberated to take courageous actions that were to change the course of world history.

Campion P. Gavaler, O.S.B.

Twelfth Sunday of Ordinary Time
Mark 4: 35–41

Gospel Summary

In Mark's gospel, Jesus is presented as one who loves to tell stories, such as the one we find in today's gospel. There are few more frightening experiences than to be in a small boat on a large body of water when a sudden squall comes up. The disciples are experienced fishermen, but they know how helpless they are in a turbulent sea.

The disciples do not understand how Jesus can be so calm at a time of mortal danger. We know, however, that in his baptism he has been empowered to deal with all kinds of chaotic situations. He has been sent by his heavenly Father to restore creation and to drive back the powers of darkness and chaos that have entered our lives through sin. He touches sick people and their health is restored; he confronts demons and they are banished; he brings peace and harmony where there had been fear and hopelessness.

Jesus has this power for good because he is in touch with the Creator who has sent him to bring to us that love which enables God to view all of creation and to declare it to be "very good" (Genesis 1: 31).

Life Implications

In our personal lives, we experience wonderful moments of peace and joy and harmony; but we also have to deal frequently with the challenge of our own kinds of chaos, such as physical ailments, mental anxiety, and all the many causes of fear and uncertainty. It is amazing how easily a "calm sea" can change into a "raging storm" of doubt, fear, and virtual helplessness.

We need to know how we, like the disciples, can call upon Jesus and suddenly find that our stormy sea becomes calm and serene. Jesus tells us that it is a matter of faith: "Why are you terrified? Do you not yet have faith?" We may be tempted to respond that we do indeed have faith for we can say "Amen" to all the statements of the Creed. That is an important kind of faith, but it is not as real and personal as the faith that God wants us to have.

The faith that calms storms in our lives is a conviction that the Risen Lord is present in our world more truly than he ever was to the disciples in Israel. This kind of faith is a special gift of God for which we must pray not only when we are in trouble but especially when things are going well. When his heavenly Father said to Jesus in his baptism: "You are my beloved Son," he was endowing him with the power of divine love that he would then offer to all of us. In effect, this is the kind of loving presence that speaks to us every moment of our lives and which can be expressed in those reassuring words that we need so much to hear: "I am with you always" (Matthew 28: 20), which means that love and trust will win out in the end.

Demetrius R. Dumm

Thirteenth Sunday in Ordinary Time
Mark 5: 21–43

Gospel Summary

Asynagogue official named Jairus pleads with Jesus to cure his daughter, who is at the point of death. While on the way to the official's house, a woman afflicted with hemorrhages for twelve years comes through the large crowd that is following Jesus, and touches his cloak. She is instantly cured. Jesus, aware that power had gone out of him, asks, "Who has touched my clothes?" The woman in fear and trembling tells him that it was she. Jesus says to her, "Daughter, your faith has saved you. Go in peace and be cured of your affliction."

While he was still speaking, people from the synagogue official's house arrive and announce that the young girl has died. Jesus says to the official, "Do not be afraid; just have faith." Taking Peter, James, and John with him, Jesus goes to the official's house. Upon arrival, the crowd ridicules him when he says that the child is asleep, not dead. He then takes the child by the hand and says to her, "Little girl, I say to you, arise!" The girl, a child of twelve, arises and walks around. Jesus gives strict orders that no one should know about what he did, and adds that the girl should be given something to eat.

Life Implications

The same Jesus, now Risen Lord, who reached out with compassion and with power to heal and to give life is with us. Gathered in his name, we pray that in our moment of affliction, we too will hear his words, "Do not be afraid; just have faith." Likewise, we pray that the Lord will extend his compassion and power through us to others who are afflicted. For one, it may be care given to an aging parent; for another, it may mean long hours spent in a laboratory searching for a cure for cancer.

Two things in today's gospel passage suggest further exploration of the mystery of Christ and its implication for anyone who wishes to follow in his way. Mark gives us the apparently need-less information that Peter, James, and John witnessed the pow-er of Jesus in raising the daughter of Jairus; secondly he tells us that Jesus gave the strange order about keeping what he had done a secret.

Jesus is quite aware of the large crowds that are beginning to follow him with the expectation that with his extraordinary power he will help them. Jesus recognizes their afflictions and responds with compassion. Yet, he must resist the temptation to reduce his mission for God's kingdom to pressing earthly afflictions like illness and hunger. He commands silence about the raising of the daughter of Jairus because he does not want the essence of his mission to be misunderstood. The fourth gospel also refers to the fact that many people misunderstood the mission of Jesus (John 6: 2,15,26).

Mark tells us that Peter, James, and John were also with Je-sus on the mountain of tranfiguration (Mark 9: 2–13) and in the garden of Gethsemane (Mark 14: 32–42): even though beloved son of God, he will be stripped of power. In consequence of his trusting obedience to his loving Father, he will suffer greatly, be treated with contempt, and be killed. Dying upon a cross, he was in fact mocked for his loss of power: "He saved others; he cannot save himself" (Mark 15: 31). Paul wrote that the message he preached, Christ crucified, is an obstacle to faith for Jews, and foolishness for the rest of us (1 Corinthians 1: 23). Yet it is in dying powerless on a cross that Jesus reveals the ultimate mean-ing of divine power as self-giving love in response to his Father's love. In this action Jesus heals the ultimate human affliction—separation from God.

Peter, James, and John, however, also witnessed the sur-prise of resurrection. Because Jesus emptied himself, becoming obedient even unto death, God greatly exalted him (Philippians 2: 5–11). No longer enjoined to be silent about what Jesus had done, they with other apostles have proclaimed the good news to the entire world. By following in the way of Jesus, each of us also as beloved son or daughter share in that life with God and with each other that no earthly affliction, death included, can destroy.

At our Eucharist today we might pray for the grace to grasp the meaning in our own lives of a truth that is as incomprehensible to human reason today as it was the day Paul wrote it: "The message of the cross is foolishness to those who are perishing, but to us who are being saved it is the power of God" (1 Corinthians 1: 18).

Campion P. Gavaler, O.S.B.

Fourteenth Sunday in Ordinary Time
Mark 6: 1-6.

Gospel Summary

It is really sad to note the attitude of Jesus' home town to their suddenly famous neighbor. On the surface, it is the usual story of how familiarity can breed contempt. They know how "ordinary" Jesus has been and they cannot allow him now to represent a world that is so much larger than their own little town. This is a strange mixture of pride and envy, with the latter seeming to take hold at Nazareth.

The tragic consequence of their refusal to abandon their provincial narrowness is that Jesus "was not able to perform any mighty deeds there, apart from curing a few sick people by laying his hands on them. He was amazed at their lack of faith." Jesus could not work more miracles there because they would not permit it! They could not open themselves to a world beyond their own safe little village. Of course, this new world that Jesus has entered is not just the world beyond Nazareth; it is the world beyond this world!

Authentic faith always expands our horizons and enriches our imagination so that we can see and yearn for that transcendent, divine world that God has planned for us. Real faith enables us to be born into a world of wonder and hope and endless possibilities. It is always tragic when we refuse to let go of our safe, little "Nazareth" and thus lose the real world of God's kingdom.

Life Implications

If we ever needed proof that Jesus was a real human being and grew up as an ordinary child it would be provided by today's gospel passage. In fact, it was his very ordinariness that scandalized his neighbors and prevented them from allowing him to be their Messiah and Savior.

However, we are dealing here with something far more dangerous than a small-town mentality. These people of Nazareth represent all of us when we want to make ourselves the measure of everything. We fear the uncontrollable world where God's gifts are to be found, and so we tend to reject anything that we cannot understand and control. We forget that all the really important things in life, such as love and happiness and life itself, are ultimately gifts to be received, not problems to be discussed and mastered. Faith gives us the courage to trust the world of God's promises and to open ourselves to these wonderful and uncontrollable realities.

When we are afraid to take such a risk, we have no choice but to defend our tiny territory and to deny everything that lies beyond it. Faith, when it is truly operative in our lives, puts us in touch with God's love and thus allows us to share the experience of Jesus who left Nazareth in order to embrace the whole world. It is the experience of God's love, discovered in the gift of our heavenly Father, that allows us to take the risk that Jesus took ... and that leads us with him, through trials and adversities, to the only world that really matters.

This "ordinary" world of ours is full of God's presence and God's promise. We need only to open our eyes. St. Paul knew this, for he wrote, "God chose the weak of the world to shame the strong" (1 Corinthians 1: 27). God can work wonders through us, just as we are, provided we trust in his love and power.

Demetrius R. Dumm, O.S.B.

Fifteenth Sunday in Ordinary Time
Mark 6: 7–13

Gospel Summary

Jesus summons the Twelve and sends them out two by two. He gives them power over unclean spirits, and instructs them to take nothing for their journey but a walking stick. He warns them about rejection: people will not always welcome them or listen to them. The disciples go out and preach repentance, drive out many demons, anoint the sick with oil and cure them.

Note that the English word "repentance" does not adequately convey the meaning of the Greek verb that Mark uses in his gospel (literally "to change the mind"). In Mark's usage the word implies a prophetic call to interpret reality in a radically new way, as from blindness to sight. "Repentance" is at once a gift and the task of turning and surrendering to God in a way that embraces every aspect of life. A New Testament example of the reality to which the word points is the conversion experience of Paul. For Paul, that radical change of direction means to live with the mind and heart of Christ (1 Corinthians 2: 6–16).

Life Implications

If you visualize Mark's dramatization of one of the most theologically significant events in his entire gospel, its comic character may strike you. It's a scene right out of the musical Godspell. Here is Jesus sending out these disciples (not the best and brightest of that society) on a mission to overthrow the reign of Satan and to proclaim the coming of God's reign. The comic aspect, if not for the disciples at least for the onlookers, is apparent when the size of the mission is juxtaposed with the means to accomplish it. The disciples, whose obtuseness and little faith Mark frequently highlights, now are instructed to go out with nothing but a walking stick—no food, no sack, no money in their belts, not even a bible.

Mark, in telling us about the beginning of the church in so dramatic a fashion, wants to be certain that disciples in his church and in our church will be mindful of some important implications. We, like the first disciples, are inadequate for the task; yet Christ's mission for God's kingdom is given to us. The comic contrast of mission and means may point to something essential about the church. If we labor under the illusion that we can bring about God's reign by our own resources, perhaps even replacing the walking stick with a sword, we will be advancing something other than God's kingdom on earth.

Paul refers to his experience of preaching the gospel not as comic, but as foolishness (1 Corinthians 1: 18–31). He relishes saying "we are fools for Christ's sake" because he understands that it is because of his weakness that the power of Christ can dwell in him (1 Corinthians 4: 10 and 2 Corinthians 12: 9). Perhaps we in the United States, who have so many of the world's resources, might reflect on the reality that in terms of accomplishing Christ's mission, all our high-tech resources should be regarded as no more than a walking stick.

At the beginning of Mark's gospel we learn that the Spirit descended upon Jesus, God's beloved Son, at his baptism by John in the Jordan. In this awareness and by the power of the Spirit, Jesus overcomes the power of Satan in the wilderness; and after John's arrest he sets out to accomplish his mission for God's kingdom. He preaches repentance, casts out unclean spirits, and cures many who are ill. By the time Mark wrote his gospel, the connection between Jesus' mission and the extension of his mission to the church was quite clear. Because disciples share the Spirit and are beloved by the Father, they also share Christ's power to preach repentance, to drive out demons, and to cure the sick.

This gospel of the Lord's commissioning disciples to carry forward his mission may remind us of our inadequacy, but paradoxically it also reminds us of our dignity and importance. God depends not only on Jesus in his humanity, but on the successors of the Twelve and on each of us to be co-creators and co-christs in bringing about a kingdom on earth as it is in heaven.

Campion P. Gavaler, O.S.B.

Sixteenth Sunday in Ordinary Time
Mark 6: 30–34

Gospel Summary

We can almost picture the disciples telling Jesus excitedly about how busy and successful they have been. They are tired now but also elated. In a contemporary setting, we might well expect Jesus to say, "Well done. Keep up the good work. In fact, you might want to pick up the pace just a little." But he says instead, "Come away by yourselves to a deserted place and rest a while."

These words of Jesus suggest something much more profound than simply, "Let's take a break." They are reminiscent of the passage in Deuteronomy where God asks Israel to keep his presence always in mind: "Take to heart these words which I command you today. Keep repeating them to your children. Recite them when you are at home and when you are away, when you lie down and when you get up" (Deuteronomy 6: 6–7). The words referred to contain the revelation about the reality of God's existence and of his passionate love for us.

As it turns out, Jesus and his disciples don't succeed in finding a respite from the crowd. But just planning to do so is already therapeutic and sets a boundary between our work in life and the equally important "remembering" of the Lord's gracious presence in our lives.

When Jesus notes that the people are like "sheep without a shepherd," he is saying, in effect, that they also need to be reminded of the primacy of God's love in their lives and of the need to feel affirmed by that love. Ultimately, it is not success at work that gives direction and meaning to life but rather it is the growing awareness of a powerful and loving One who asks us to come aside and bask in a Presence that truly makes life worthwhile.

Life Implications

The gospel story seems at first to suggest that we should separate ourselves from our work at times in order to find some peace and quiet. That is surely part of it, but something much more profound is at issue here. We must in fact find the quiet place in our hearts to which we can withdraw at any time, whether at work or at play.

It is in this quiet place that we first heard the baptismal words, "You are my beloved child," for these words of God, our loving Father, are spoken to all of us, just as they were to Jesus. They are spoken softly but very insistently. When we take time to hear them in that quiet place in our hearts, there is nowhere else that we would rather be, for they affirm us and liberate us to be all that we are meant to be. And when this happens, we are no longer like "sheep without a shepherd," no longer confused about the meaning of life or about our ability to live in peace and joy.

One may object that, if this happens, we will soon be "out of touch" or distracted or living in fantasy. But that is exactly what does not happen. For when we are thus in touch with God, we become far more attuned to what is real in life than do the so-called "practical people." The worst of all illusions is to think that it is normal to be a creature who has lost all contact with the Creator. The ideal situation is to be slightly distracted by the awareness of God's love and thus to be calmly focused on the task at hand. This "benign" distraction is really a way to be in prayerful contact with God ... and with reality.

Demetrius R. Dumm, O.S.B.

Seventeenth Sunday in Ordinary Time
John 6: 1–15

Gospel Summary

Because of the signs Jesus was performing on the sick, a large crowd followed him as he went up on a mountain with his disciples. When Jesus saw the crowd, he said, "Where can we buy enough food for them to eat?" Philip answered, in effect, that he did not know. Another disciple said to Jesus, "There is a boy here who has five barley loaves and two fish; but what good are these for so many?" Jesus had all the people recline. Then he took the bread, gave thanks, and gave it to the people, and also as much of the fish as they wanted. After the banquet, the disciples gathered twelve baskets with fragments from the five barley loaves that were left over. Since the people wanted to carry him off and make him king, Jesus withdrew to be alone on the mountain.

Life Implications

We can readily identify with the disciples' feeling of helplessness in the situation. The gospel is not about a reasonable response of compassion extended to a few people in need. Rather, it is about having no resources to match the needs of a huge crowd of people we do not even know. There is no difficulty in recognizing this situation in our own world. About every four seconds someone dies of hunger … 75 percent are children. The shocking statistic suggests the image of an avalanche, impossible to stop and imperative to flee.

There are in fact many ways to distance ourselves from the countless people who are hungry and from the implications of this gospel. We can hurry on to the rest of this chapter in John's gospel, and devote ourselves to reflection about Jesus as the bread of life that satisfies our deepest spiritual hunger for eternal life. As spectators, we can reduce the mass of hungry people to the status of virtual reality on a screen. We can succumb to a kind of idolatry when we believe that absolute laws of the economy make it impossible for all people to have work, basic health care, and enough food to live.

The life implication of this gospel is simple: Jesus wants to work the miracle of feeding a huge number of people who are hungry; but the miracle will not happen without someone to provide five barley loaves and two fish. Jesus must have loved the boy who was willing to share what was really his to eat. The miracle of the gospel is as much about the boy as it is about Jesus. And today the boy is each of us who has something to offer the Lord. Jesus does not spiritualize the hunger of the poor, or postpone his love for them to the next world.

Dom Helder Camara, a Brazilian bishop, once said, "When I feed the poor they call me a saint. When I ask why so many people are poor they call me a communist." Today the Lord asks all sorts of people who have influence in shaping public policy to make their contribution by keeping Helder Camara's question in the forefront of debate about political, social, and economic policies. The contribution of those who seek solutions to the very difficult question of Helder Camara is as essential as the contribution of those who are daily engaged in the immediate relief of starving people. And regardless of the effort, there will always be the feeling: but what good is this among so many?

If God gave us the natural resources, the brains, and the will to achieve what we have in our country through science and technology, it is likely that with Christ we can also bring about the miracle of every child of God having enough to eat. Jesus feels so deeply about this that he said if someone is hungry, it is he himself who is hungry (Matthew 25: 31–46). As we celebrate our Eucharist today, let us recall the truth that Jesus is present in the total reality of his Body. The Body of Christ includes a large number of poor people. All are dear to him. Can we celebrate the Eucharist authentically and be indifferent to their plight?

Campion P. Gavaler, O.S.B.

Eighteenth Sunday in Ordinary Time
John 6: 24–35

Gospel Summary

Today's gospel passage is taken from the Bread of Life Discourse in John's gospel. The first verses presuppose that we know about the miracle of the multiplication of loaves and fish that has just been described (John 6: 1–15). At this point, there is a serious disconnect between Jesus and those who have witnessed that miracle. They see only the spectacular nature of the miracle whereas Jesus wants them to see that this is really a preparation for discovering in him the true and only sufficient source of nourishment: the "food that endures for eternal life" (John 6: 27).

The crowd does not catch the meaning of Jesus and so they ask what God expects of them. They no doubt expect to be told about observances that will please God. But Jesus poses a far more difficult challenge. They are now expected to "believe in the one he sent" (John 6: 29). Faith in Jesus and acceptance of his teaching is the primary requirement. And when they ask for a sign like the manna given to Israel in the desert, Jesus states his claim as the new manna that gives perfect nourishment: "I am the bread of life; whoever comes to me will never hunger, and whoever believes in me will never thirst" (John 6: 35).

Life Implications

It is important to note that, though Jesus identifies himself as "the bread of life" (John 6: 35), he is not yet speaking about the sacramental Eucharist. The emphasis in this segment of the Bread of Life Discourse is placed on the faith-acceptance of the teaching of Jesus. In other words, he is nourishment first of all as one who offers us the life-giving words of God about the meaning of our lives. Moreover, this divine message, if it is to nourish for eternal life, must be accepted in a way that leads us from self-centeredness to unselfish love and sacrifice for others.

It is for this reason that Jesus states that he is the bread of life for the one who "comes" to him and "believes" in him (John 6: 35). There is no reference yet to eating or drinking, which will come later. It is very important to understand this point because it reminds us that only a believing reception of the Body and Blood of Jesus will bring us true life. Unfortunately, it is only too easy to receive the Eucharist without a true and effective commitment in our daily lives to the ideal of unselfish behavior that is so perfectly represented by this sacrament.

To put the matter another way, we are being challenged by Jesus to avoid a magical or mechanical understanding of the power of this supreme sacrament. It does not nourish us spiritually simply by the action of receiving it. There must also be a firm intention to change one's life in a way that is in harmony with this supreme Sacrament of Jesus' giving of himself for us.

Demetrius R. Dumm, O.S.B.

Nineteenth Sunday in Ordinary Time
John 6: 41–51

Gospel Summary

The Jews murmured about Jesus because he said, "I am the living bread that came down from heaven." (In John's gospel, "Jews" is often a technical term meaning the religious authorities who are hostile to Jesus. Thus, for example, Jesus and his disciples, all Jews, would not be "Jews" in this restricted sense.) Those who were hostile to Jesus argued that he was from earth, not from heaven. Wasn't he the son of Joseph? Jesus then proclaims that he is from heaven and that God is his Father. Further, he says that anyone who is taught by his Father and drawn to his Son will believe and have eternal life. Jesus then begins his discourse on the Eucharist: "I am the bread of life ... whoever eats this bread will live forever; and the bread that I will give is my flesh for the life of the world."

Life Implications

Hunger for life is at the heart of this passage from the bread-of-life chapter of John's gospel. The experience of hunger provides a revelation of the most fundamental truth of human existence. We are incomplete, totally dependent on things and others outside of ourselves. From the moment of receiving life at conception, we are hungry. If our need is not satisfied even for a short time, we die. As we grow to adulthood our hunger for more life seems to be without limit. We desire good food and drink, shelter, wealth, knowledge, health, medical care, a healthful environment, social status, loving companions. At times we may even eat from the tree of forbidden fruit in the illusory desire for a human life without limits. Jesus responded to the hunger of people for life—he cured the sick and he fed a huge multitude. The people responded by coming to take him away and make him king. Whereupon, Jesus fled to be alone (John 6: 1–15). He was well aware of our need for the necessities of life; however, he recognized a deeper hunger that could not be satisfied by bread alone. This gospel testifies that Jesus revealed himself as the bread from heaven that will satisfy the deepest human hunger for life. The number of people who saw and heard Jesus in the flesh was quite small. John addresses his gospel to his own community and to us who have not seen and heard Jesus, yet have the same deep hunger for life as those who did. We, like John's community, hear the good news from the Risen Lord sacramentally at a Eucharistic meal in which he gives himself to us as the bread of life.

When Jesus revealed himself as the bread from heaven, many did not believe him. It was plain to see that he was from earth: "Is this not Jesus, the son of Joseph?" Because many refused to believe that Jesus himself was the living bread come down from heaven, they refused to believe that Jesus could give himself as the bread of the Eucharist for the life of the world. When we hear the revelation of Jesus in the gospel, we too might be tempted to refuse belief, saying something like the following: Were not these words written by a human being like us? Is this not ordinary bread, made from wheat like any other bread?

We, like the people who heard Jesus speak, cannot with our reason alone recognize him as the bread from heaven. The good news of the gospel is that the Father that gives us this bread draws us in and teaches us. This is the gift of faith that enables us to see that it is Jesus, given by the Father, who will satisfy our deepest hunger for eternal life. Because the gospel is proclaimed to all, we believe God loved the world so much that he gave his only Son so that the hunger of every human being may be satisfied.

What does it mean to say that one who believes has eternal life? The Father reveals the meaning of eternal life as drawing us out of love to Jesus, his gift of bread to us for our life (read Hosea 11: 4). Jesus reveals the meaning of eternal life by defining himself as bread given for the life of others. To have eternal life means to share in the self-giving love of the Father and Jesus. "God is love ... we love because he first loved us" (1 John 4: 16–19). Etty Hillesum, a young Jewish woman who was executed after volunteering to be taken to a concentration camp in place of others, also captured the meaning of life as giving herself as bread for others. Shortly before her death in Auschwitz in 1943, she wrote: "I have my body like bread and shared it ... and why not; they were hungry, and had gone without for so long."

Campion P. Gavaler, O.S.B.

Twentieth Sunday in Ordinary Time
John 6: 51–58

Gospel Summary

The eight verses that constitute today's gospel reading represent the climax of the lengthy Bread of Life Discourse in Chapter six of John's gospel. The first fifty verses have been concerned with the spiritual nourishment that Jesus has brought into our spiritually famished world. In fact, Jesus declares, in verse 35, that he is "the bread of life," that is, the nourishment that provides the kind of spiritual life that cannot be threatened by illness or death. He makes it clear, however, that this nourishment is available only to those who believe in him, that is, to those who accept and adopt in their lives his teaching about unselfish love.

In the climactic verse fifty-one, we find the first mention of the Eucharist itself: "the bread that I will give is my flesh for the life of the world." This verse, therefore, represents John's version of the institution of the Eucharist, which is found here in his gospel rather than at the Last Supper. This radical change gives John ample opportunity to insist, in the previous fifty verses, on the importance of a believing, rather than a merely routine, reception of the Eucharist.

Life Implications

John uses much more graphic language than the other evangelists in his description of the institution and the implications of the Eucharist. When the audience of Jesus resists his statement about his "flesh for the life of the world," he repeats and reinforces his original words: "Amen, amen, I say to you, unless you eat the flesh of the Son of Man and drink his blood, you do not have life within you" (John 6: 53).

This forceful statement not only insists on the importance of receiving the Eucharist but it also means, as we see everywhere in this gospel, that the meaning of the Eucharist must be reflected in the lives of those who receive the sacrament. For this is Body-broken and Blood-poured-out for others. Accordingly, we will participate fully in the benefits of the Eucharist only to the extent that we imitate, in all aspects of our lives, the generosity and unselfishness that we see in the life of Jesus himself. The Eucharist will certainly help us to be more thoughtful and compassionate and forgiving but this cannot happen without our own serious commitment to love and service of others.

John then goes beyond the other gospels in spelling out the practical implications of conforming our lives to the demands of the Eucharist. The most significant consequence is presented in verse 57: "Just as the living Father sent me and I have life because of the Father, so also the one who feeds on me will have life because of me." This is a truly daring and wonderful assurance that we fragile human beings can hope to share in the very life of God. We can actually enter into that flow of life that courses between the Father, Son, and Holy Spirit. And to the extent that this happens, through our commitment to God's unselfish way of loving, our eternal life will be assured.

Demetrius R. Dumm, O.S.B.

Twenty-first Sunday in Ordinary Time
John 6: 60–69

Gospel Summary

This passage brings the sixth chapter of John's gospel to a climactic conclusion. Jesus has fed a large crowd with bread and fish; he has revealed his divine identity as I AM by showing his power over the sea; in the synagogue at Capernaum he has revealed that he himself is the bread of life given by the Father—as the bread of his teaching and as bread of the Eucharist. Now upon completion of his teaching, many of his followers murmured, saying, "This saying is hard; who can accept it?" Jesus responds that human nature alone (the "flesh") is of no avail in coming to believe and to have life in him. This faith and life is possible only as a gift of the Father.

After the exchange in the synagogue, many of his disciples left him. Jesus said to the Twelve, "Do you also want to leave?" Simon Peter answered, "Master to whom shall we go? You have the words of eternal life. We have come to believe and are convinced that you are the Holy One of God."

Life Implications

Faith and life in Jesus is a gift beyond human expectation and understanding. This is the implication not only of this passage but of John's entire gospel. "For God so loved the world that he gave his only Son, so that everyone who believes in him might not perish but might have eternal life" (John 3: 16). The gift of eternal life is NOW; it does not begin after we die. In faith we can live without fear: "Even though I walk through the valley of the shadow of death, I will fear no evil, for you are with me" (Psalms 23: 4). The saints of every age witness to the reality that faith is participation in the joy, the prayer, the gratitude of Christ's life now: "Rejoice always. Pray without ceasing. In all circumstances give thanks, for this is the will of God for you in Christ Jesus" (1 Thessalonians 5: 16–18).

Today we hear the good news that the Risen Lord is present among us sacramentally as the bread of life given by the Father—as the bread of his teaching and as bread of the Eucharist. We too may be inclined to murmur, "This saying is hard; who can accept it?" Our gospel passage does not tell us why many of his followers refused to believe Jesus and left him. We do know, however, the countless factors in our own culture that dissuade us from giving ourselves to the Lord in faith. Suffering is often experienced as incompatible with God's love. Our "subjective-value" culture reduces faith to no more than "religious preference." Nobel Prize winners tell us there is no God. There are likewise moral decisions that lead to belief or away from belief. After her lecture at a university, a student asked Flannery O'Connor how he could be certain that God exists. She replied, "Give alms." Jesus himself said, "How can you believe, when you accept praise from one another and do not seek the praise that comes from the only God" (John 5: 44)?

Today's gospel passage alerts us to the fact that faith is not primarily assent to a creed about God but a personal covenant with God. Like friendship, faith is mutual self-giving; it can become stronger or become weaker; it can begin and it can end. Jesus emphasizes the radically personal nature of faith by using the word "betray" and by asking whether the Twelve will also decide "to leave" him. Jesus knows that the human commitment of faith is not so steadfast as God's commitment. He knows that his refusal to let the people make him king (John 6: 15) and Judas' love of money (John 12: 6) will lead to a loss of faith in him and to betrayal.

In the Last Supper Discourse Jesus knows that the faith of his followers will be tested again, not by his teaching as in the synagogue at Capernaum but by his death on a cross. "Do you believe now? Behold, the hour is coming and has arrived when each of you will be scattered to his own home and you will leave me alone" (John 16: 31–32). His followers of weak faith did leave him—Judas betrayed him, Peter denied that he had ever known him. The story of Judas and Peter is both a warning and a source of hope. Like Judas, we too can finally choose to place ultimate, suicidal trust in something other than God. Like Peter, we too may grievously sin; yet trust that if we return, the Lord will welcome us with the joy of steadfast love.

Campion P. Gavaler, O.S.B.

Twenty-second Sunday in Ordinary Time
Mark 7: 1–8, 14–15, 21–23

Gospel Summary

Today's gospel reading introduces a familiar theme concerning religious observance. The Pharisees were a group of very observant Jews whose very name means in Hebrew the "separated ones." They were declared different because they were so meticulous in their concern for even the finest details of the Mosaic Law. In fact, they even added prescriptions to this religious Law which, according to Jesus, made it burdensome and thus compromised its very purpose, which was to liberate also from the bondage of scrupulosity and spiritual pride. This is what Jesus means when he speaks of their "human traditions" which have distorted the Law.

Jesus comes into conflict with the Pharisees, not because he undervalues the Jewish Law, but because he understands that this Law is primarily about love and freedom, and that its ritual elements are all subordinate to this primary concern. The danger in all ritual observance is that it can foster pride and lead to a sense of superiority in contrast to those who seem less observant. The result is self-righteousness and a tendency to be judgmental in regard to others.

Jesus does not condemn ritual observance, which today would mean frequenting the sacraments and devotion to prayer. What he does condemn is a religious observance that is limited to the external aspects and does not include that for which the rituals exist, namely, conversion of one's heart from pride and self-centeredness to loving concern and compassion for others. Since this kind of conversion is a gift from God, there is no reason for pride in achieving it.

Life Implications

In our secularized world, many are not concerned at all about either ritual observance or conversion of heart. When things are going well, there seems to be no need for God, much less religious observance. This gospel message may seem irrelevant to such as these. However, reality will inevitably place all of us in a situation of need and, when that happens, we can only hope that we have the good sense to turn to God with humility and trust.

The gospel speaks directly to those of us who are in fact serious about the requirements of religious observance. For us, the Pharisees serve as clear examples of the grave danger of careful but superficial observance. We may be scrupulously concerned with all kinds of pious practices, some indeed of our own devising. But at the same time we may be seriously lacking in compassion and forgiveness. We may very well be, like the Pharisees, self-righteous and judgmental. Such a situation provides us with the illusion of virtue but it is in fact far removed from the deep personal conversion preached by Jesus.

Conversion of the heart means that we have discovered that all our goodness comes from the love of God for us. This leads to genuine prayer of praise and gratitude as well as a real yearning to share this gift with others. It is such persons who will excel in generosity and tolerance and thoughtfulness. And in their praise and gratitude they will truly fulfill the ideals of the divine Law.

Demetrius R. Dumm, O.S.B.

Twenty-third Sunday in Ordinary Time
Mark 7: 31–37

Gospel Summary

Jesus leaves the district of Tyre, and by way of Sidon goes into the district of the Decapolis. People beg him to cure a deaf man with a speech impediment. Jesus puts his finger into the man's ears, touches the man's tongue with his spittle, looks up to heaven, groans, and heals the man, saying, "Ephphatha!" (that is, "Be opened!") The people are astonished and say, "He has done all things well. He makes the deaf hear and [the] mute speak."

Life Implications

Mark's gospel is filled with false expectations, misunderstandings, and rejections of Jesus not only among the people he encounters, but among his own disciples as well. The disciples, even Peter, do not see and do not hear with complete faith, and thus say things that indicate blindness and deafness to the identity and meaning of Jesus. This characteristic of the gospel fits very well with the ancient tradition that Mark wrote his gospel in response to the experience of the church in Rome during the period around A.D. 70. Things were not working out as expected.

The church by this time had been separated from the Jewish community; persecution had heightened under the emperor Nero; Peter and Paul had been executed; the expected return of the Risen Lord to destroy the power of Satan was not happening. Disappointed people were leaving a church that was proclaiming a savior apparently powerless to overcome the evil they were experiencing. Mark realizes that many Christians in that stressful experience did not see, did not hear, did not speak with the power of Christ—their faith was not Christian faith. To address this situation desperately in need of redemption, Mark wrote his gospel in such a way as to highlight the fact that even the first, eye-witness disciples also had false expectations that Jesus did not meet.

Mark's narrative about the past proclaims the good news today that Jesus has the power to heal our deafness and our blindness so we can speak the truth about him and glorify God without impediment. The power of faith's hearing and seeing enables us to realize that the only way to share Christ's resurrection is through sharing Christ's love, thereby following in his way of the cross. It is only the power of love that conquers evil.

Mark introduces the healing of the deaf man with the speech impediment by telling us that Jesus had left the district of Tyre and went by way of Sidon into the district of Decapolis. Mark does not explain the odd itinerary—it would be like saying that Jesus went from Pittsburgh to Atlanta by way of Buffalo. Note that he had introduced the previous unit in his gospel about the Gentile woman's faith by telling us that she lived in the district of Tyre. The woman clearly got the better of Jesus in their sharp exchange about whether his ministry extended beyond his own Jewish people to the Gentiles. Mark makes a point of reporting that Jesus, in admiration of her faith, did drive the demon out of the woman's daughter, and immediately went into the district peopled by Gentiles.

Jesus heard God speaking to him through the voice of the Gentile woman that the ministry of divine love is to be extended not only to the Jews, but also to the Gentiles. Now among the Gentiles Jesus hears the people who plead for the cure of the deaf man with a speech impediment. He looks up to heaven, seeing that all his healing power comes from God, and groaning with compassion he speaks the words of love, "Be opened." Today at our Eucharist we pray for the gift of sharing the faith and compassion of Christ—hearing, seeing, speaking with the power of his Spirit in the particular circumstances of our own lives.

Campion P. Gavaler, O.S.B.

Twenty-fourth Sunday in Ordinary Time
Mark 8: 27–35

Gospel Summary

Today's gospel passage gives us an account of the most critical turning-point in the public ministry of Jesus. The stage is set by the seemingly innocent questions of Jesus about his identity. Peter speaks for all the disciples when he declares confidently, "You are the Messiah." In view of the miracles of Jesus in Galilee that would seem to be an obvious conclusion.

Jesus, however, is deeply disturbed by this answer and the reason is immediately revealed: "He began to teach them that the Son of Man must suffer greatly..." The clear implication is that he is not a Messiah in the political sense that the disciples understood. He is not interested in leading them into a war of liberation from the Romans, but hopes instead to liberate them in a far more radical way from the bondage of sin and death.

Peter's strong reaction and the rebuke by Jesus should be understood as a moment of crisis when Peter is challenged to abandon human wisdom and to accept the divine way of doing things. It may be helpful to note that the word Satan had the original meaning of any "adversary" before it came to be the name of the great adversary of God. Accordingly, Jesus is asking Peter to avoid being his adversary but rather to stand with him in the difficult time of his suffering and death.

This challenge to Peter reminds us of the words of Isaiah: "For my thoughts are not your thoughts, nor are your ways my ways—oracle of the Lord. For as the heavens are higher than the earth, so are my ways higher than your ways, my thoughts higher than your thoughts" (Isaiah 55: 8–9).

Life Implications

One of the most difficult challenges in the life of a Christian is the need to move from a life guided by human wisdom to the acceptance of God's way of doing things. There is nothing wrong with human wisdom and it is certainly preferable to human folly. We need to make good and reasonable and prudent decisions in life. "Dropping out" of life is not a very good way to change things for the better.

Nonetheless, human wisdom is not an absolute reality and must therefore be subservient to a higher divine wisdom. From the teaching of Jesus, we discover that the purpose of human life is not just to acquire wealth and power but rather to direct all such human success to the divine purpose of love and service. Jesus clearly manifested human wisdom in the power and eloquence that he displayed in the early days of his ministry. However, as today's gospel reminds us, he let go of all that in order to love in a way that meant suffering and even death.

All this may seem to be a severe prescription for human life. However, it is important to distinguish the suffering that loving entails from all other kinds of suffering. There is literally a world of difference between them. The suffering that comes from loving leads to genuine happiness—a happiness that is far more satisfying than the pleasure that comes from having one's own way most of the time.

And since such unselfish loving puts us in touch with God's own love, it leads also to the final liberation that we call resurrection. Good Friday is not nearly as bad as it looks from the outside; and Easter Sunday is much better than we can ever imagine.

Demetrius R. Dumm, O.S.B.

Twenty-fifth Sunday in Ordinary Time
Mark 9: 30–37

Gospel Summary

While journeying through Galilee, Jesus teaches his disciples and tells them that he is to be handed over to those who will kill him, and after three days he will rise. The disciples do not understand what he is talking about. When they come to Capernaum, Jesus asks them what they were arguing about on the way. They remain silent because they were discussing among themselves who was the greatest. Jesus calls the Twelve together and says to them, "If anyone wishes to be first, he shall be the last of all and the servant of all." Then Jesus takes a child and putting his arms around it says, "Whoever receives one child such as this in my name, receives me; and whoever receives me, receives not me but the One who sent me."

Life Implications

The second reading of Mass from the Letter of James describes an unredeemed situation of the time when James wrote his letter and of our own time: "For where jealousy and selfish ambition exist, there is disorder ... You covet but do not possess. You kill and envy but you cannot obtain; you fight and wage war." (James 3: 16, 4: 2) This would also serve as a description of the situation that Jesus addresses in today's gospel passage. Humanity continues on a journey with the Lord; and we are still arguing and fighting among ourselves about which one of us is the greatest.

Our culture's understanding of greatness comes down to amassing enough wealth and power to do whatever you want. Jesus, on the other hand, reveals that human greatness has to do with living the truth of our relationship with God and with each other regardless of how much wealth or power we may possess.

The secret of understanding the greatness of Jesus and thereby the meaning of human greatness is to understand the relationship of Jesus with God. He reveals what it means to live and to die as God's beloved Son (Mark 1: 11). In other words, Jesus shows us the implications of being created in the image and likeness of God as beloved son or beloved daughter. Believing in his human soul that his relationship with God was his ultimate truth, Jesus trusted that God's will for him amidst the trials he endured could only be love.

Jesus once said to his disciples, "Amen, I say to you, whoever says to this mountain, 'Be lifted up and thrown into the sea,' and does not doubt in his heart but believes that what he says will happen, it shall be done for him" (Mark 11: 23). Through total trust, a finite human being comes into harmony with the infinite God who has the power to create mountains. It is in that trust that Jesus could pray in the face of imminent death, "Abba, Father, all things are possible to you. Take this cup away from me, but not what I will but what you will" (Mark 14: 36). He trusted that his loving Father, who has power to create life, would prevail over the power of death.

Jesus also reveals that our relationship with God is inseparable from our relationship with each other. To give oneself to God as Jesus did means to be in complete harmony with God's creative love for every human being and for all creation. Mark tells us that the disciples were discussing among themselves on the way who was the greatest. Jesus, who as God's servant would soon give up his life for us, said to them, "If anyone wishes to be first, he shall be the last of all and the servant of all."

The creative service of love unites God, Jesus in his humanity, and every human being in the most intimate communion of life. Jesus says, "Whoever receives one child such as this in my name, receives me; and whoever receives me, receives not me but the One who sent me." Only by following in the way of Jesus will we be on the path to greatness according to God's wisdom, and thereby ourselves often be prompted to deeds of sacrifice and love.

Campion P. Gavaler, O.S.B.

Twenty-sixth Sunday in Ordinary Time
Mark 9: 38–43, 45, 47–48

Gospel Summary

M ark's gospel is noted for its use of plain and blunt language, and today's gospel passage is a good example of that. John and his brother James were called "sons of thunder" (Mark 3: 17) because of their impulsive natures and this is manifested here again when John wishes to stop those outsiders who are using Jesus' name in their exorcisms. Jesus, however, rebukes John with the reminder that he is here to love and to heal; he is not interested in copyrights or credits.

Jesus then speaks forcefully about what really constitutes sinfulness and where one's passion should come into play. It is scandal that should arouse our indignation. This means taking advantage of vulnerable people who can so easily be exploited when they should be protected and assisted. These are obviously children, but all vulnerable persons of whatever age are included. This is where real sinfulness lies and the punishment is swift and severe. Gehenna was the place where Jerusalem's trash was deposited. It was usually smoldering and was infested by all sorts of vermin. It was certainly not where one would hope to end up.

Life Implications

The failure to distinguish between major and minor sinfulness is a special danger in the way in which we organize our priorities in life. It is all too easy to be more concerned about appearances and reputation than about the far greater sinfulness of racism or sexism or other kinds of deep-seated prejudice.

All religions have a tendency to claim exclusive control of the avenues of salvation. But God is surely free to work outside of our familiar religious structures also. This doesn't mean that such structures are unnecessary or unimportant. It does mean that we should work in genuine humility to make our own religious structures as open as possible to the saving power of God.

Scandal is often thought to be behavior that shocks people by departing from traditional patterns. The emphasis is placed on the exceptional nature of the scandalous person's actions. We see in today's gospel that this is not what Jesus meant by scandal. For him, scandal occurs when we use actions or words to mislead and deceive those who are not able to understand what is happening. Thus, a person who holds a position of trust can easily take advantage of those who rely on his or her authority or influence. This is so sinful because it destroys the very fabric of trust, which makes community life possible.

In a certain sense, one can also scandalize oneself by pursuing limited goals and thus endangering the real purpose of life. It is not wrong to seek wealth or power or knowledge, but all these goals must be made subordinate to the goal of eternal life. In other words, they must be placed under the control of unselfish love. Otherwise, the "eye" or the "hand" can become more important than life itself, with disastrous consequences. The language here seems harsh because so much is at stake. Actually, it means exactly what is intended by the frequent gospel references to gaining one's life in this world but losing it forever.

Demetrius R. Dumm, O.S.B.

Twenty-seventh Sunday in Ordinary Time
Mark 10: 2–16

Gospel Summary

Some Pharisees, wanting to involve Jesus in current controversies about divorce, ask him whether it is lawful for a husband to divorce his wife. Jesus replies that only because of the hardness of the human heart, Moses permitted a husband to write a bill of divorce and dismiss his wife. At the beginning, however, God created humans, male and female, to be joined together as one in marriage. Jesus says that what God has joined together, a man cannot separate by writing a bill of divorce. And if he attempts to do so and marries another woman after dismissing his wife, he commits adultery.

People were bringing children to Jesus so that he might touch and bless them, but the disciples rebuked them. When Jesus saw this, he became indignant and said that the kingdom of God belongs to such as these children. And furthermore, whoever does not accept the kingdom of God like a child will not enter it. Then he embraced the children and blessed them.

Life Implications

If we do not hear a homily as good news leading to thanksgiving and hope, it means that we are missing something essential in the text or context of the gospel passage. In the present passage, the point is not that Jesus is making a more severe law about marriage, but that he is continuing to proclaim the good news of God's kingdom. This central proclamation of Jesus' mission means the possibility of a new kind of human existence for those who accept God's reign, including men and women who enter marriage. To suggest what the experience of God's reign in marriage would be like, Jesus recalls God's dream of how a man and woman could live together as one in a beautiful garden created for their delight.

Today against the background of tragic divorce statistics and the feeling among many that marriage is only a human, social construction to be defined any way we please, the saying of Jesus about Garden-of-Eden marriage sounds like an impossible dream. Jesus indicates that in our fallen state, it is an impossible dream. The kingdom he promises is a free, divine gift as much as the original kingdom at the beginning of creation. Only those enter who come and accept God's gift like a child.

Our gospel passage today may be experienced as good news if we follow the lead of Jesus by praying for a deeper awareness and trust that God creates us for love and happiness. The Genesis story of creation that Jesus refers to tells us of the wonderful harmony that God intended for men and women to enjoy as equal partners in marriage. The text of Genesis does not describe their delight when the man and woman discovered that they were suitable partners for each other, except that they were "both naked, yet they felt no shame" (Genesis 2: 25).

A small book of the Bible, the Song of Songs, is a lyrical love poem that completes the story begun in Genesis, and thus gives us a deeper sense of God's intention in creating human beings capable of enduring love. In the Song we have a description of the beauties of their bodies as the man and woman discover each other. We also have a description of the unspoiled beauties of nature, fresh from the hand of the Creator: roses, lilies, fig trees, cedars, palm trees, pomegranates, dates, honey, wine, gazelles, turtledoves, sheep, horses.

The innocently erotic images of the Song of Songs describing without shame the loving relationship of the young man and woman were soon extended to describe the marriage covenant of Israel with God, and later by Christians to describe the union of the Church with Christ. For the Jewish people, the Song came to be associated with the Passover feast; for Christians, the Song was used in the baptismal liturgy. Many saints have used the Song's images to describe the mystical experience of union with God.

God's creative love for us has not changed because we have eaten forbidden fruit and our hearts have become hardened. The good news that Jesus proclaims is that God's dream can become real again not only for men and women in marriage but for all of us. In Jesus' proclamation, the beginning-time of harmony and delight is also the hoped for end-time of God's reign, already present now for those who will accept it with childlike faith.

Campion P. Gavaler, O.S.B.

Twenty-eighth Sunday in Ordinary Time
Mark 10: 17–30

Gospel Summary:

In today's gospel passage, the rich young man who approaches Jesus asks the universally felt human question about the possibility of reaching a life beyond death. In other words, why do we humans have such a strong yearning for life and are nonetheless created mortal? This young man is obviously very confident and he uses ingratiating language as he addresses Jesus. When Jesus replies that only God is good, he is simply stating a truism of the Jewish tradition.

Jesus then reminds this young man of the traditional teaching in the Ten Commandments about the kind of moral behavior that promises eternal life. The young man replies in effect: "Been there, done that!" Jesus in turn seems to be captivated by his self-confidence and tells him that there is indeed more to be done if he really is serious about eternal life.

This more sublime ideal requires an unburdening of oneself in order to be free to follow Jesus wholeheartedly. This sobers up the rich young man immediately for he cannot imagine a life of security without possessions. Jesus then tells his disciples that reaching the kingdom of heaven will be hard for everyone, rich or poor, because attachment to possessions is not just a problem for the wealthy. The challenge therefore does not come from the size of one's bank account but rather from the degree of one's attention to God and of one's generosity in living the challenge presented by Jesus.

Life Implications:

When Jesus declares that it is easier for a camel to pass through the eye of a needle than for a rich person to be saved, he is using a strong metaphor to emphasize the difficulty of paying proper attention to God when one is encumbered by the attachments and distractions involved with possessions. It takes much time and effort to acquire possessions, and even more time to care for them, to protect them, and to enjoy them. This fact establishes a kind of competition between one's attention to God and one's concern for the management of one's earthly affairs.

This matter receives much more attention in Luke's gospel. He came from Antioch and had personal experience of the extremes of wealth and poverty in that pagan city. The parable of the rich man and Lazarus (Luke 16: 19–31) is a good example of his concern about the way in which possessions tend to blind a person to the lasting values in life. Nowhere in this parable is there any suggestion that the rich man had acquired his wealth immorally. He is condemned simply because his preoccupation with his possessions has blinded him to the fact that Lazarus was in his backyard begging for food.

The clear implication is that the amount of one's possessions is not nearly as dangerous as is the degree of one's attachment to them. To be liberated from the drugging influence of possessions is to be ready to put the needs of others before one's own comfort and convenience. It was Saint Augustine who said that, from a Christian perspective, the surplus of the wealthy belongs to the poor. And surplus means all that is not required for a modest lifestyle. I think he would apply that standard to wealthy nations also.

Demetrius R. Dumm, O.S.B.

Twenty-ninth Sunday in Ordinary Time
Mark 10: 35–45

Gospel Summary

James and John ask that when Jesus enters his glory he would grant them positions of honor and power. Jesus responds that they do not understand the cost of what they are asking. When the ten hear about the ambitious request, they become indignant. Jesus then summons the Twelve and reveals the meaning of the divine mission for the kingdom that he has come to fulfill. Those who are rulers over the Gentiles lord it over them and make their authority felt. Among his disciples, however, whoever wishes to be great will become a servant, and whoever wishes to be first will be the slave of all. Then follows perhaps the most radical and most revealing saying of Jesus about himself and about discipleship in the entire gospel: "For the Son of Man did not come to be served but to serve and to give his life as a ransom for many."

Life Implications

Peter, James, and John are especially close to Jesus. They are with Jesus on the mountain of Transfiguration and in the garden of Gethsemane. In these turning points of his life, Jesus sees clearly that his commitment to do his Father's will would entail suffering and death. Peter, James, and John (representing all of us) do not see how the failure of suffering and death could have anything to do with God's plan. In this gospel James and John are more concerned with the success of having highest positions of honor and power in the kingdom. Shortly before, Jesus had called Peter a Satan because Peter rebuked him when he began to talk about the suffering and death he would soon undergo.

It is obvious why Mark immediately after the episode of this gospel tells us about the blind beggar, Bartimaeus. We are all blind when it comes to seeing what Jesus is talking about because his teaching is so contrary to our instinctively self-centered way of understanding the meaning of being the greatest and being first. When we hear the words of Jesus, we may even feel the instinct to ignore them as foolish and impractical in our world. We can only ask for the grace to recognize our blindness and to pray with the blind beggar: "Jesus, Son of David, have pity on me … I want to see." Only when we see with the seeing of faith can we follow Jesus on the way to the glory God has prepared for him and for us.

When we pray for the miracle of understanding the meaning of our lives in the way that Jesus understood the meaning of his life, we are seeking to know what it means to be "servant" in the unique particularity of each of our lives. The beauty and completeness of God's kingdom will not be realized without the unique service of each disciple, regardless of how exalted or how lowly the service may be in the eyes of the world. What is essential to see is that the service Jesus invites us to do is the way of love.

To be servants in the way that Jesus was servant means to live in complete trust that God loves us in the way that God loved Jesus during his earthly life. Jesus was not servant out of servile fear of a tyrant Father, but as beloved Son, who in turn loved as he was loved. It is a free service of love, not of fear. When the Apostle Paul was cured of his blindness, he was able to say in a letter to the Christians of Ephesus: "… be imitators of God … and live in love, as Christ loved us and handed himself over as a sacrificial offering to God …" (Ephesians 5: 1–2) And to the Galatians he wrote: "… I live by faith in the Son of God who has loved me and given himself up for me … you were called for freedom … do not use this freedom as an opportunity for the flesh; rather, serve one another through love … But if you go on biting and devouring one another, beware that you are not consumed by one another." (Galatians 2: 20, 5: 13–15)

Campion P. Gavaler, O.S.B.

Thirtieth Sunday in Ordinary Time
Mark 10: 46–52

Gospel Summary:

The curing of a blind man in today's gospel passage is re-markable for several reasons. First of all, it is quite unusu-al in the gospels to give a name to the person healed, and this suggests that Bartimaeus was a recognizable member of the early Christian community from which Mark's gospel came.

Secondly, the blind man refers to Jesus as "son of David," a clearly Messianic title, but Jesus does not correct him, as he does elsewhere in Mark's gospel out of concern that he be seen as a political Messiah. No doubt the fact that he has by now made it clear that "the Son of man must suffer greatly" (Mark 8: 31), there is less danger of mistaking him for one who will lead them in a war of liberation against the Romans.

Finally, it is worth noting that this is the last miracle of Jesus in Mark's gospel prior to his death and resurrection. As such, it forms a kind of book-end with another curing of a blind man in Chapter 8, verse 22ff. This may very well be intended as a way of highlighting the Transfiguration of Jesus (Mark 9: 2ff). These blind men receive their sight just as Jesus is illuminat-ed as he discovers the full meaning of his messianic mission. He has been sent to save the world through his loving rather than through violence. In all three cases, though in very different ways, an enlightenment is portrayed. This suggests that the real cure of blindness, for Bartimaeus and for all of us, involves a dis-covery of the true purpose of our human existence, namely, that we, like Jesus, must "die" for others by loving them to the end.

Life Implications:

All of the miracles of Jesus have symbolic as well as historical significance. They certainly have an historical basis and certainly did establish the credibility of Jesus for those who were open-minded. At the same time, they represent the healing through

Jesus of various spiritual maladies. Christians of all ages are in danger of spiritual blindness because they do not "see" that human life is primarily for loving concern and not for acquiring power or for building monuments. Jesus also cured paralytics, whose muscles were non-functional, just as he is prepared to heal the far more dangerous spiritual paralysis of cynicism and negativity. In a similar way, Jesus is prepared to "drive out the demons" in our lives by helping us to experience the presence of God and thus to be delivered from the chaos of a life of confusion and disorientation.

Of course, there are many who are too "practical" to allow for this kind of divine influence in their lives. They are represented by the crowd in today's gospel who "rebuked" the blind man, telling him to be silent. We note with wonder that they nonetheless respond to Jesus' command to "call him" by saying to Bartimaeus, "Take courage; get up, he is calling you." We would all be much happier people if we also could bring ourselves, in faith, to offer this same encouragement to the people in need whom we meet every day.

Demetrius R. Dumm, O.S.B.

Thirty-first Sunday in Ordinary Time
Mark 12: 28–34

Gospel Summary

In a friendly conversation a scribe asks Jesus what he believes the first of all the commandments to be. Jesus replies by quoting from a prayer that the scribe, he himself, and every faithful Jew would recite every day from memory: "Hear, O Israel! The Lord our God is Lord alone! You shall love the Lord your God with all your heart, with all your soul, with all your mind, and with all your strength." To this commandment Jesus then immediately joins a commandment from Leviticus 19: 18: "You shall love your neighbor as yourself." When the scribe expresses agreement with understanding, Jesus says to him: "You are not far from the kingdom of God." Mark adds that no one dared to ask Jesus any more questions.

Life Implications

After reading dozens of pages in the various biblical dictionaries, one wishes that someone had dared to ask Jesus what he meant when he said, "You are not far from the kingdom of God." The expression "kingdom of God" appears more than 150 times in the New Testament. It not only points to the mystery of Jesus, God incarnate, but also to the mystery of human communion in divine life now and at the end-time. A recent declaration of the Congregation for the Doctrine of Faith ("Dominus Iesus") states that the meaning of the kingdom of God both in Sacred Scripture and in documents of the Catholic tradition is not always exactly the same.

With the disclaimer that the divine-human reality cannot fully be contained by human concepts, the kingdom of God seems to include three principal aspects: (1) God's plan and saving presence in history, not as a tyrant, but to invite all of us to loving communion in divine life; (2) the human acceptance of the divine gift through conversion in childlike faith and gratitude; and

(3) the realm of life with God in and through the Church, fully to be realized only at the end-time.

Except for spatial proximity, the life implication of Jesus' saying "You are not far from the kingdom of God" is the same for us as it was for the scribe. Jesus himself is the saving presence of God inviting all of us to loving communion in divine life. Is it possible for us to respond by loving God with all our heart, all our soul, all our mind, all our strength, and to love our neighbors as ourselves? It is possible only if we remember through the gift of faith that God in every moment of our life loves us with a total, personal love.

To the command that we must respond to God's love with total love, Jesus adds the command that we must love our neighbors as ourselves. The conjunction of the two commandments is already present in the Exodus tradition into which Jesus grew up. As a response to the love that was given to them through their liberation from slavery, the Israelites must never forget God's word to them: "... you shall love the alien as yourself; for you too were once aliens in the land of Egypt" (Leviticus 19: 34). A graphic statement in the First Letter of John forcefully reminds us that we must never forget the meaning of Jesus' words to the scribe of today's gospel and to us: "If anyone says, 'I love God,' but hates his brother, he is a liar ..." (John 4: 20).

The Spirit enabled Jesus perfectly to realize the kingdom of God in himself by accepting the Father's infinite love, by responding to that love in total trust and obedience, and by loving his neighbors even to giving up his life. When we pray "thy kingdom come" in our Eucharist today, we ask that the Spirit will bring about the realization of God's plan and loving presence in us and in each of our neighbors.

Campion P. Gavaler, O.S.B.

Thirty-second Sunday in Ordinary Time
Mark 12: 38–44

Gospel Summary

The Scribes mentioned in today's gospel were not a religious sect, as were the Pharisees and Sadducees. They were simply men who knew how to read and write—a distinct minority in those days. Illiterate people depended on them for help in preparing documents, such as contracts, and this gave them considerable power and prestige in the community. But it also tempted them to become proud and to consider themselves above the laws that govern ordinary people.

It is important to note that Jesus does not condemn them because they are more learned than most. They deserve condemnation only because their pride leads them to unjust behavior. Being able to control judicial processes enabled them to defraud vulnerable people, such as widows.

In the second half of the gospel passage, we note a contrast between the heartless Scribes, who prey on widows, and a poor widow who puts them to shame because of her generosity. Her "widow's mite" is proportionately far more generous than larger and ostentatious gifts given out of abundance. Others give from their surplus, while she gives from her livelihood. Nor does she seek in any way to advertise her piety.

Life Implications

In our world, knowledge is so readily available that we often do not realize what a precious possession it is. There is real power in knowledge and this kind of power, like power in general, can be very corrupting. Such abuse of knowledge occurs when it leads to pride, to odious comparisons with less favored persons, and even to abuses, such as sharp dealings and other forms of injustice. We know also how easy it is for the more learned to take advantage of the naive and vulnerable ones. Such "white collar crime" is rarely punished adequately ... but God knows who is guilty.

On the other hand, knowledge can be used in very helpful and positive ways. Good teachers have a precious opportunity to deliver people from the very real bondage of ignorance. I know from personal experience how gratifying it is to see a listless student begin suddenly to grasp the importance of learning and then to blossom into one who becomes hungry for knowledge. This is truly like finding a treasure in a field, which leads to profound gratitude on the part of a student empowered in this way to explore a world of wonderful opportunities.

Wealth is even more obviously a form of power. It can be abused through avarice and greed, but it can also provide a wonderful opportunity for service. The generosity of wealthy persons can liberate less-fortunate ones from the bondage of misery and insecurity. Investing in the poor is a most wise and provident use of one's resources.

The Scribes had some knowledge and wealth, but that was of little value to them in the end. The simple, poor widow turned out to have chosen the path to supreme knowledge and wealth beyond measure.

Demetrius R. Dumm, O.S.B.

Thirty-third Sunday in Ordinary Time

Mark 13: 24–32

Gospel Summary

Jesus promises his disciples that they will see the Son of Man coming in the clouds with great power and glory. The angels will gather his elect from the four winds. His coming in glory will be preceded by tribulation. The sun will be darkened, the moon will not give its light, the stars will fall from the sky, and the powers in heaven will be shaken. These will be signs just as fig leaves sprouting are a sign that summer is near. Jesus adds that their generation will not pass away until all these things take place. Though heaven and earth will pass away, his words will not pass away. Then Jesus says: "But of that day or hour, no one knows, neither the angels in heaven, nor the Son, but only the Father."

Life Implications

Jesus speaks of the ultimate triumph of his future coming with great power and glory immediately before what appears to be his ultimate defeat without any power and glory—dying like a criminal on a cross. This would seem to be a foolhardy promise to his disciples on Jesus' part unless we understand the source of his unconquerable hope. Does a man on his way to the electric chair make promises about what he will do in the future?

From the very beginning of Mark's gospel we learn that Jesus the beloved Son will devote his life to bringing about the kingdom of God. Through Jesus, God's power will overthrow the earthly reign of Satan. Satan will attempt to thwart the divine plan through lifelong temptation of Jesus. Jesus, however, remains faithful to his mission, and casts out many demons from those under the power of Satan.

In response to the accusation that he expels demons with the help of the prince of demons, Jesus says that if that were true, the kingdom of Satan would be divided against itself. Luke in his gospel presents Jesus' understanding of his mission in similar terms: "But if it is by the finger of God that [I] drive out demons then the kingdom of God has come upon you" (Luke 11: 20). Jesus also indicates the cosmic nature of the power of God's kingdom when the disciples reported that in his name they had power over the demons: "I have observed Satan fall like lightning from the sky" (Luke 10: 18).

Here is the source of the unconquerable hope that Jesus proclaims in the face of the apparent triumph of Satan's reign through those who are about to kill him. Jesus trusts that just as God's kingdom has come to earth through him, the kingdom's ultimate triumph will also be accomplished through him.

Today we pray for the gift of receiving the Spirit of Jesus, and thereby the grace of unconquerable hope. For one who has received his Spirit, there is no hopeless situation—the power of God's reign is supreme on earth as it is in heaven. Death itself, apparently Satan's triumph over us as over Jesus, cannot defeat the supreme power of God's love. Saint Paul reminds us: "For he must reign until he has put all enemies under his feet. The last enemy to be destroyed is death" (1 Corinthians 15: 25–26).

In seeking the life implications of Christ's promise to come in power and glory at the end-time, we should also note the corresponding passage in the gospel according to Matthew. Like Mark, Matthew tells us that Jesus spoke of his coming in power and glory when his death was imminent. In Matthew's gospel, however, Jesus is very specific about identifying the elect who will be gathered by the angels from the four winds. The criterion for entry into God's kingdom is so radical in its simplicity: "… whatever you did for one of these least brothers [or sisters] of mine, you did for me … what you did not do for one of these least ones, you did not do for me" (Matthew 25: 31–46).

Campion P. Gavaler, O.S.B.

Solemnities of the Lord During Ordinary Time

Trinity Sunday, Cycle B
Matthew 28: 16–20

Gospel Summary

This carefully crafted passage is the climactic summary of the essential themes of Matthew's gospel. Jesus, now Risen Lord, reveals that all power in heaven and on earth has been given to him, and thus he has authority to commission his disciples to continue and to extend his mission to all the nations of the earth.

Jesus' epiphany and commission to the eleven take place on a mountain, the symbolic place where humans encounter the divine presence. The mountains of encounter unite in a single narrative the biblical covenants, and make all history a sacred history. These awesome places of the divine presence evoke the memory of crucial turning points of human history: Ararat, Moriah, Sinai, Zion, Carmel. Matthew, fully in harmony with this tradition, brings the narrative of the divine plan to its climax. He tells of Jesus' trial of temptations, his sermon, and his transfiguration on a mountain. From the severe testing of faith on the Mount of Olives, Jesus descends to suffer and die in obedience to his Father's will.

Now on a mountain, Jesus with divine authority commissions the eleven to make disciples of all nations, baptizing them in the name of the Father, and of the Son, and of the Holy Spirit. God's promise to Abraham after the testing of faith on Mount Moriah will at last be fulfilled. Through Jesus, son of Abraham, "all the nations of the earth will find blessing" (Genesis 22: 1–18). All nations will hear the good news, and be taught to observe what the Lord has commanded. Matthew concludes his gospel and begins the era of the church with the promise of Jesus: "And behold, I am with you always, until the end of the age."

Life Implications

The good news we hear proclaimed on Trinity Sunday is that Jesus the Risen Lord wants us to share divine life with him in the oneness of intimate, familial love with his Father and Holy Spirit. Through the gift of baptism we belong to God, and God belongs to us. With Jesus we can say Our Father. We are at home in God.

To be certain that we do not imagine the era of the church to be an illusory Utopia above the ambiguities of the human condition, Matthew interjects a surprising note of realism. He tells us that though the eleven disciples recognize Jesus as Risen Lord and worship him, at the same time they doubt. He uses the same Greek verb for "doubt" as he did when Jesus stretched out his hand to Peter, frightened and sinking in the stormy water: "O you of little faith, why did you doubt?" (Matthew 14: 22–33)

A theme of Matthew's gospel is the contrast between the total, single-minded faith of Jesus and the double-minded, little faith of his disciples. Jesus tells the disciples that because of their little faith they do not understand him, and for the same reason they are unable to cast out a demon (Matthew 16: 8 and 17: 20).

The disciples, except for one of the original Twelve, are willing to follow Jesus and listen to his commands; but at the same time their "common sense" tells them that what Jesus expects is way beyond their capacity to accomplish. It is not difficult for us present-day disciples to identify with the feeling of inadequacy and doubt in the face of the powerful forces that oppose the fulfillment of the divine promise of blessedness in our own circumstances. Like the first disciples, we worship the Risen Lord; and we doubt. Yet we go on because we trust with our little faith that all power in heaven and on earth has been given to Jesus.

The Risen Lord, who conquered even death, is with us as he promised. When we do not understand what is going on, when the demons in us and around us seem invincible, when we begin to sink in the stormy water, when the task at hand seems too much for us, Jesus stretches out his hand and says: "O you of little faith, why did you doubt?" With our little faith, we can only respond: "Lord, I believe; help my unbelief."

Campion P. Gavaler, O.S.B.

The Body and Blood of Christ, Cycle B
Mark 14: 12–16 and 22–26

Gospel Summary

The Sacrament of the Body and Blood of Christ, which we call the Eucharist, is not just one of the seven Sacraments. It is the supreme Christian Sacrament and it is presented as such in all the Gospels. Mark makes it clear that Jesus instituted this Sacrament during a Passover meal, which in turn re-enacts the central Exodus event in the history of Israel. For Jesus, this Sacrament interprets his own dying and rising as the definitive Exodus—the supreme act of liberation from bondage— now intended for all people and for all time. This represents for us, therefore, the ultimate liberation from sin and death ... and therefore from the bondage of guilt and fear and despair.

In this profoundly symbolic action at the Last Supper, Jesus reveals to his disciples the meaning of his imminent death and resurrection. He will not be dying as a misguided idealist, who loses everything at the end and who is believed by some naïve persons to have been somehow victorious. Rather, he is one who freely gives his life for others and whose love leads directly to his resurrection, since God cannot ignore such generous and unselfish love.

The earlier readings in today's liturgy, taken from the Book of Exodus and the Letter to the Hebrews, make it clear that participation in this Sacrament implies a solemn covenant, by which we commit ourselves to the kind of unselfish love that we see in the life and death of Jesus.

Life Implications

It is important to take seriously the words of Jesus about the reality of his presence among us in the Eucharist. It is a mistake, however, to think that the profound symbolic meaning of this Sacrament is in any way incompatible with its reality as the very Body and Blood of the Lord. In fact, if the reality alone is emphasized, there is always the danger of a simplistic and magical understanding of this Sacrament.

When we truly appreciate the symbolic and universal meaning of the Eucharist, we will see it, not only as the supreme example of the love of Jesus, but also as a claim on all who receive it to make that unselfish love the central feature of their own lives. In other words, we must by all means reverence this Sacrament and receive it with great devotion, but it is even more important to live its meaning when we return to our workaday lives. Receiving the Body and Blood of the Lord and continuing to be self-centered and insensitive at home or at work is clearly a serious contradiction.

It is very difficult, of course, to be truly and consistently dedicated to unselfish service. When we receive the Eucharist with profound awareness of its true meaning we experience the reality of God's love for us and, as that experience deepens, we become ever more free to be the kind of loving presence in our world that Jesus calls us to be.

The importance of all this becomes clear when we realize that our participation in the victory of Jesus will ultimately depend on how well we have lived his message of love and concern for others. In other words, in the end it will be the quality of our loving that will be decisive and not just the frequency of our reception of the Eucharist. It is precisely that dedication to unselfishness in all we do that will enable us to join Jesus in his glorious resurrection. Honoring and receiving the Eucharist will surely help us to live in that way, but it is our loving care and concern for others that will make the Eucharist victorious in our lives.

Demetrius R. Dumm, O.S.B.

Feast of Christ the King, Cycle B
John 18: 33b–37

Gospel Summary

The choice of this text from John's gospel could not be more appropriate for the feast of Christ the King. It is taken from the Passion Narrative and is part of the exchange between Pilate and Jesus during his trial before the Roman Procurator. This trial scene is particularly important for John, and he devotes no less than twenty-nine verses to it. In fact, this scene reveals John's concept of the central issue in the life and ministry of Jesus.

When Pilate and Jesus discuss the question of kingship, it is clear that Pilate has in mind political and military power. He also knows that he, as a representative of the mighty Roman Empire, possesses this kind of power in fullest measure. He lives in a palace and has access to the finest military forces of those days. By contrast, Jesus stands before him as a shackled and helpless prisoner. The contrast could not be more obvious.

Nevertheless, when Jesus says that he has come into this world to "testify to the truth," he is claiming a power that directly challenges the power of Pilate. For the truth to which Jesus is testifying is not philosophical or scientific truth, but the ultimate truth about God's intention in creating us human beings. Jesus has received this truth from his heavenly Father and reveals it in his words and actions ... and never more so than during his passion and death.

This revelation offers a truth that is so revolutionary that we could never believe it without the witness of Jesus and the gift of faith. Jesus is telling us nothing less than that the only truly effective and lasting power in the world is that of unselfish love. He is a bound prisoner because he loves others and he will soon give his very life for love of them. This love of Jesus will conquer the hearts of millions, while the power of Pilate and the great Roman Empire will crumble to dust.

Life Implication

The message in today's gospel is that truly revolutionary message, given to us by Jesus, which permeates all the gospels. It is a difficult message because we find it so hard to believe that quiet, gentle, and persistent love, which seeks only the good of others, can possibly be more powerful than all the money and missiles on which we rely for security.

We can comprehend and trust this teaching only by the gift of faith. But we must remember also that this precious gift is offered to everyone by the love of God. Accordingly, we need to be open to all the many ways in which God's love is made available to us—through contact with God in prayer, but also through the love of other good people, and even through the beauty of nature.

As we gratefully embrace this goodness in life, in spite of much evil there also, we will gradually become free enough to dare to trust the power that is in our unconditional loving. We do not need to live in mansions or command armies or be endowed with special gifts in order to be a loving presence in our world. Yet we can be certain that such loving has the potential to transform the universe. Jesus is indeed the King of kings and Lord of lords, but only because of his great love of us.

Demetrius R. Dumm, O.S.B.

Feasts of Mary and Saints

Solemnity of the Immaculate Conception
Luke 1: 26–38

Gospel Summary:

Theologians often make a distinction between "high" Christology, which emphasizes the divine nature of Jesus, and "low" Christology, which emphasizes his human nature. This distinction finds a parallel in the case of Mary. Today's feast would belong to "high" Mariology, because it celebrates a special privilege of Mary which flows from her status as Mother of God. Most New Testament references to Mary, however, belong to "low" Mariology because they begin with a very human Mary responding to the initiative of the angel Gabriel.

This does not in any way detract from the importance of the Immaculate Conception of Mary, which celebrates the fact that she was without sin from the first moment of her conception. However, it does remind us that this wonderful privilege was granted to her by anticipation of her future status as mother of Jesus and, therefore, of God.

It is important to note that, as today's gospel makes clear, Mary's status as mother of God presupposes her response to the angel Gabriel with that magnificent expression of love and trust and generosity: "Behold, I am the handmaid of the Lord. May it be done to me according to your word" (Luke 1: 38). All the privileges of Mary derive from this moment of unconditional self-surrender to the plans of God. It should not surprise us, therefore, to see that the gospel of Luke devotes more attention to the Annunciation than to any other event of Mary's life.

Life Implications:

The sinless condition of Mary, from the beginning to the end of her life, elicits our admiration and prompts us to be grateful to God for making this possible in one who shares our nature as human beings. Although we certainly cannot imitate her sinless condition, we can be greatly encouraged by this signal victory over evil. We live in a world of so much sin and violence that we are tempted to wonder whether the light really can overcome the darkness, as John's Prologue promises (John 1: 5). But we are immensely reassured as we celebrate each year this victory of Mary, "our tainted nature's solitary boast" (William Wordsworth).

At the same time, we need to remember that this victory came directly from the willingness of Mary to accept a mysterious mission from God which, as she surely must have suspected, would lead to grievous suffering. We too need to make difficult choices that may demand much love and courage. And we too are aware that it may be very painful to remain faithful to the choices that God expects of us. In such situations, the generosity of Mary remains a wonderful model for us. Moreover, we can be sure that her maternal solicitude will accompany us as we try to live in accordance with our best instincts.

When we reflect upon the fact that sin is the worst kind of bondage, the sinless Mary is recognized also as the only one among us human beings who is truly free. Those who aspire to freedom solely through the acquisition of power should pause to consider that the ultimate freedom of Mary came through her resolute and loving obedience to the mission that God offered to her. She became a model of freedom through her loving generosity, and this will always be the only truly effective way to acquire human freedom and dignity.

Demetrius R. Dumm, O.S.B.

Solemnity of Mary Mother of God
Luke 2: 16–21

Gospel Summary

Today's gospel text suffers somewhat from being removed from its biblical context. We are told that the shepherds "went with haste and found Mary and Joseph, and the infant lying in the manger." It is helpful to note that they did this only because they had received a vision of angels who told them, "This will be a sign for you: you will find an infant wrapped in swaddling clothes and lying in a manger" (Luke 2: 12). The shepherds are thus taken out of their workaday worlds and asked to see their lives in a new and wonderful way.

The insistence on the image of an "infant wrapped in swaddling clothes," that is, wrapped in warm flannel, alerts us to a profound symbolism here, for the flannel bands stand for God's loving care which is shown to us in the coming of Jesus as our Savior. In a very real sense, we can say that God has wrapped the whole world in secure and loving bands by sending his beloved Son to us as an embodiment of endless loving kindness.

Since this feast is the feast of "Mary Mother of God," it is important to note also that "Mary kept all these things, reflecting on them in her heart." We are not told what "all these things" might be, but we can rest assured that they embraced the whole wonderful experience of bearing a child who is already destined to change the course of human history in ways that will be revealed only later—ways that will involve both painful self-sacrifice and glorious victory.

Life Implications

The beginning of a new year provides us with an opportunity to reflect on the special gift of time. We recall the events of the previous year and express our gratitude for all the good things that have happened, all the while being aware that there have also been sad and painful and perhaps sinful realities. But most of all we celebrate the promise of a new set of months and we try to be hopeful in spite of threats of war and recession and just growing older.

Today's gospel has a special message for us as we hang up the new calendar with mixed feelings. The fresh new year is in some ways like the infant Jesus "wrapped in swaddling clothes and lying in a manger." Both the new year and the new child seem so vulnerable, but the almighty power of God is hidden in the new year, just as it is in the tiny infant. God is fully prepared to wrap our fragile lives and hopes in the warm blanket of his ever-present and constant love. With such assurance, we can face the future with generous hope and with light hearts. For we too need to realize that the angels who spoke to the shepherds are speaking to us also when they say, "This will be a sign for you: you will find an infant wrapped in swaddling clothes and lying in a manger." Come, let us adore him.

Demetrius R. Dumm, O.S.B.

Saints Peter and Paul, Apostles
Matthew 16: 13–19

Gospel Summary

In his gospel Matthew establishes an inseparable link between the identity of Jesus and the meaning of the church. Further, Matthew affirms that the identity of Jesus and the meaning of the church are inseparable from the action of the heavenly Father. Simon from a revelation of the heavenly Father, not from flesh and blood, confesses Jesus to be "the Messiah, the Son of the living God." In response, Jesus confers upon Simon a new title, the Rock. Upon Simon, the Rock, Jesus, the Christ, promises to build his church. The gates of hell, Jesus further promises, shall not prevail against it. And to Simon Peter (from petra, the Greek word for "rock"), Jesus gives the keys to the kingdom of heaven with authority to "bind and loose" with divine sanction in the universal church (my church). On this feast of Peter and Paul, one should note Paul's affirmation that the heavenly Father, not flesh and blood, also revealed Jesus as Son to him (Galatians 1: 16).

Life Implications

In order to appreciate the lasting significance of the saints in the Catholic faith-tradition, we have to see the saints in relation to Christ, and thereby in relation to the Father and the Holy Spirit. It is through the creative action of the Spirit that we can see the saints as members of the church in divine-human personal communion. In this context we can then look at the unique personalities of the saints and examine their unique roles in actualizing Christ's mission in the world.

Peter certainly has both a unique personality and a unique role in actualizing Christ's mission in the world. Christ gives him his role as the solid Rock upon which he will build his church. However, Christ also calls him a rock that might cause him to stumble. By trying to talk Jesus out of following his heavenly Father's will, Peter becomes an agent of Satan (Matthew 16: 21–23). It is no surprise that history teaches us that this characterization of Jesus applies not only to Peter, but Peter's successors as well. Christ continues to build his church upon the popes, Peter's successors as bishops of Rome; but like Peter they too at times can be like rocks on the road. Christ, however, does not permit evil to prevail over his church despite our human failings.

The gospels make no attempt to whitewash Peter's failures: he boasted about his loyalty to Jesus, but then denied him three times with curses. Despite his glaring weaknesses, you get the feeling from the gospel accounts that Jesus was fond of this rough-and-ready, uneducated fisherman. Peter was a constant, sometimes helpful companion in the crucial events of Jesus' life. After the threefold "Do you love me?" Jesus, now Risen Lord, says to Peter, "Feed my sheep" (John 21: 15–17). Acts of the Apostles tells the story of Peter's unique role in the early church as chief shepherd who cares for Christ's flock.

If Peter denied Christ three times with curses, Paul persecuted the Body of Christ with great zeal. Then one day on the road to Damascus, he heard those life-changing words "Saul, Saul, why do you persecute me?" When Paul asked for the identity of the voice, he heard, "I am Jesus whom you are persecuting." From that moment of faith's recognition, Paul completely identified with the person of Jesus and his apostolic mission for the salvation of the world.

The lasting significance of Peter and Paul is that they are witnesses to the Lord's resurrection. To believe that Jesus is truly risen and alive in us is possible only as a gift of the Holy Spirit (1 John 3: 24). The resurrection of Jesus, Saint Thomas Aquinas teaches us, is beyond the power of human reason to prove or to disprove. Human reason ("flesh and blood") at most can offer only arguments for or against the reality of the resurrection. Yet, our affirmation of faith is from the solid ground that human reason provides. The historical testimony of Peter and Paul supports our faith not only because they proclaimed the Lord's resurrection, but because they gave their lives in martyrdom. Today, we pray to share in the gift of Peter and Paul's faith, and promise—despite our own failings—to be witnesses to the Lord's resurrection by our good works of love.

Campion P. Gavaler, O.S.B.

Birth of John the Baptist, Cycle B
Luke 1: 57–66, 80

Gospel Summary

Luke introduces his gospel narrative of Jesus with the events surrounding the birth of John the Baptist. In prior verses related to our passage, we learn that a priest Zechariah and his wife Elizabeth have no children, both being well advanced in years. While Zechariah is performing his priestly duty in the sanctuary of the temple, an angel appears and says to him that Elizabeth will bear a son who was to be called John. But because Zechariah did not believe, and questioned the angel, he became unable to speak. After Elizabeth did give birth to a son, Zechariah wrote on a tablet, "John is his name." Immediately his tongue was freed and he spoke, blessing God. The child (whose name means "Yahweh has shown favor") grew and became strong in spirit, for he was to become a prophet of the Most High.

Life Implications

The unbreakable bond between the Jewish people and the people of the new covenant in God's plan of salvation is clearly evident in today's feast. It is from the Jewish people that John the Baptist, Mary, and Jesus are born so that the tender mercy of God will visit all people. It is from the Jewish people that the church receives the revelation of the most fundamental truths of faith. In the words of the Second Vatican Council, the church continues to draw "sustenance from the root of that well-cultivated olive tree onto which have been grafted the wild shoots, the Gentiles."

The most fundamental truth from which we draw sustenance is that God is present in human history as one who extends to us the favor of merciful love. We also learn from the Jewish people that the mystery of divine presence is beyond comprehension. The "I AM" of the divine name is a name beyond names (Exodus 3: 14 and John 8: 58). A child born of aged Abraham and Sarah or a bush that burns but is not consumed before Moses signals a presence beyond human understanding and control.

It is precisely because the mystery of the divine presence is beyond comprehension that the decision to trust or not to trust is inevitable for every one of us. Zechariah, upon hearing the outlandish words of the Lord's angel, did not trust and became mute, unable to speak a word (Luke 1: 20). Luke immediately afterward tells us that the Virgin Mary, too, was not able to understand the promise of the Lord's angel. However, her response "How can this be, since I have no relations with a man?" (Luke 1: 34) is asked out of trust, not out of doubt. The mystery even of human friendship can deal with a thousand difficulties and questions that are asked out of trust, but is deeply wounded by even one question asked out of doubt.

To receive the gift of recognizing the divine presence through faith calls forth a wholehearted response. The essence of that response is not only to trust, but also to bless God with praise and gratitude. When Zechariah wrote on the tablet "John is his name" immediately his mouth was opened and he spoke a blessing "because of the tender mercy of our God by which the daybreak from on high will visit us to shine on those who sit in darkness and death's shadow, to guide our feet into the path of peace" (Luke 1: 68–79). Mary's canticle of praise and gratitude in response to the favor of divine presence is one of the most beautiful blessings of the entire biblical tradition (Luke 1: 46–55).

Today's feast celebrating the birth of John the Baptist reminds us to pray again for the faith to recognize the divine presence in our lives, to trust in God's tender mercy with an undivided heart, and to bless God always and everywhere with a glad and grateful heart. Further, in the difficult circumstances that life brings to us all, only as a grateful expression of trust that God's will is to love us can we with confidence pray, "Thy will be done."

Campion P. Gavaler, O.S.B.

Assumption of the Blessed Virgin Mary
Luke 1: 39–56

Gospel Summary

Today's gospel offers us once again the beautiful story of Mary's visit to her cousin, Elizabeth, who is pregnant with John the Baptist. This act of thoughtful concern brings great joy to Elizabeth, sensed even by the child in her womb, but the highlight of the story is the hymn of praise and thanksgiving that Mary offers in her "Magnificat."

This splendid hymn transcends time and space as it sings of God's goodness and mercy to Mary and to all of us, in every place and at all times. In spite of the real and tragic presence of evil and sorrow in our world, the dark clouds of violence cannot hide the reality of God's love and concern for all the "lowly" ones. They have not been abandoned and their oppression at the hands of the "arrogant of mind and heart" will not last forever.

Life Implications

The victory that is celebrated in Mary's "Magnificat" is expressed in today's feast of the Assumption of Mary into heaven. Though the Scriptures do not explicitly refer to this event, it is implicit everywhere in the promise that God will "lift up" and give glory to all of us who, like Mary, trust in his goodness and obey his commandments.

The high and mighty ones of this world, who rely on power to serve their purposes, are inclined to ridicule those who accept the wisdom of Jesus and do their best to be a loving, caring presence in a much too violent world. Their way seems foolish and unpromising, but God is on their side and their ultimate victory is assured. Mary's glorious Assumption into heaven is celebrated, therefore, as the victory of love over hatred, of mercy over cruelty, and of gentleness over violence.

Unfortunately, in a society where sheer power is too often assumed to be the only means for getting things done, we are tempted to abandon the wisdom of Jesus. Indeed, we feel help-less in dealing with violence in our homes and in our streets. That is why this feast of the Assumption is so important, since it provides us with an opportunity to reaffirm our faith in God's promises. God really does remember his promises to Abraham and therefore to all of us believers, who are spiritual children of that great patriarch, whom Paul calls "the father of all of us" (Romans 4: 16). God really does intend to "lift up the lowly" and to "fill the hungry with good things." And if that is so, we should gladly sing with Mary, "My soul proclaims the greatness of the Lord; my spirit rejoices in God my Savior."

Demetrius R. Dumm, O.S.B.

Feast of All Saints
Matthew 5: 1–12

Gospel Summary

For the feast of All Saints we are asked to reflect on the first, and perhaps most important, verses of Matthew's Sermon on the Mount. These verses have come to be called the Beatitudes. Since Matthew's Sermon on the Mount represents the moral ideals taught by Jesus, it is most appropriate to ponder their implications when we honor all the saints, that is, those who lived those ideals in an exemplary way.

The Beatitudes strike the keynote for all of the teaching that follows in the three lengthy chapters that make up the Sermon on the Mount. It is also true that the first Beatitude offers a key to the meaning of the seven remaining Beatitudes in Matthew's account.

The decisive word in this first Beatitude is the word "poor." Its meaning is derived from a Hebrew word meaning "an afflicted one." This name was applied to those Jews of the immediate pre-Christian era who were economically and politically powerless, but who continued to hope in God even though he seemed to have abandoned them. They were often poor in the sense of destitute, but their more basic poverty was in terms of power and control.

Jesus makes the daring statement that these downtrodden ones should in fact be declared blessed, that is, fortunate. What could possibly justify such a radical and apparently nonsensical conclusion? Jesus certainly does not intend to bless powerlessness as such. However, he does affirm the blessedness of those who, because they are powerless, are saved from the illusion that worldly power can in fact give us the only truly important and lasting gifts, such as, love, happiness, and life itself. Being delivered from that fateful illusion, they are free to turn to God, who is ready and willing to give them the Kingdom—something that earthly goods could never provide! It is therefore an attitude of humility and trust in the presence of God.

Life Implications

The ideal presented here must not be mistaken for a misguided passivity or timidity in the presence of the challenges of this life. Rather, it liberates us from self-centered and self-serving efforts, which will ultimately prove unproductive, so that we may be present to others in a loving, caring, and helpful way. This is summed up neatly in the seemingly paradoxical but very true statement, "The only gift we can keep is the one we give away!" Or, in gospel language, "What profit is there for one to gain the whole world and forfeit his life?" (Mark 8: 36)

The remaining seven Beatitudes are in a sense echoes of this primary one. Those who "mourn" are those who have dared to become vulnerable through loving. The "meek" have renounced power and violence as a means of acquiring happiness ... and thus find happiness! Those who "hunger and thirst for righteousness" have a passion for the reforms that will enable everyone to live and dream. Those who are "merciful" renounce anger and vengeance as they offer forgiveness. The "clean of heart" are the sincere and truthful ones who reject all that is mere sham and pretense in life.

The "peacemakers" promote forgiveness and reconciliation as the only sure way to peace. And those who are "persecuted" are those who persevere in the pursuit of these ideals in spite of ridicule from others who seem to be wise and prudent. Thus, the Beatitudes represent a radical but reliable program for true holiness ... as illustrated in the lives of that great army of saints whom we honor today.

Demetrius R. Dumm, O.S.B.

Dedication of the Lateran Basilica in Rome
John 2: 13–22

Gospel Summary

In order to celebrate the annual festival of Passover, Jesus goes up to Jerusalem. After he enters the temple area, he drives out those who are selling oxen, sheep, and doves, as well as the money changers, saying, "Stop making my Father's house a marketplace." When challenged to defend his outrageous action, Jesus replies, "Destroy this temple and in three days I will raise it up." His hearers think he is speaking of the temple in Jerusalem, which had been under construction for forty-six years. Only after Jesus rose from death did his disciples realize that he had spoken about the temple of his body.

Life Implications

The Basilica of Saint John Lateran in Rome symbolizes a crucial turning point in the long and remarkable history of the Catholic Church. The basilica was once a palace belonging to the Lateran family, dating back at least to the time of the persecution of Emperor Nero (A.D. 54–68). Emperor Constantine made a gift of the building to Pope Melchiade about the year 311. Before Constantine's rule, Christians were a persecuted sect struggling for survival within the hostile Roman Empire with its temples dedicated to the worship of many gods. The Lateran palace became the papal cathedral and the papal residence for more than a thousand years, despite being ravaged by the Vandals, by fires, and by earthquakes. Our parish churches may rightfully look to this cathedral church of the Bishop of Rome as their mother church. Its feast of dedication also may remind us of our spiritual bond with our brothers and sisters in many countries where Christians may not worship in public and are persecuted as an outlawed sect.

In today's gospel Jesus refers to the temple in Jerusalem as "my Father's house." That the invisible God manifests his presence in visible signs recognizable by faith is at the heart of biblical revelation. The opening hymn of Genesis celebrates the creation of the entire universe as the construction of a beautiful temple in which God dwells and may be glorified. God continues the revelation of divine presence not only in the universe and in the events of history, but in human structures—in the ark of the covenant leading the Jewish people through the wilderness, and in the temple Solomon built in Jerusalem.

In Jesus, revelation that God lives among us in visible signs reaches its climax. Jesus is the temple in which "the whole fullness of the deity dwells" (Colossians 2: 9). The theme of the divine presence in the universe, in the events of history, in human structures, and in Jesus is extended as in a rich tapestry even further. Jesus identifies his body with the new temple promised in messianic times, and in turn his body is identified with the Church and with each individual member of the Church. "Do you not know that you are the temple of God, and that the Spirit of God dwells in you" (1 Corinthians 3: 16, also read Ephesians 2: 19–22).

The Book of Revelation completes the theme of "temple and divine presence" to the fullest imaginable depth. In the end time of eternity, all earthly temples will be no more because God will be the temple. "I saw no temple in the city, for its temple is the Lord God almighty and the Lamb" (Revelation 21: 22). Now we are temples because God lives in us. Then, God will be the temple because we will live in him. Annie Dillard once remarked, "Home is the name of God." Because this is true, our faith can also help us have a new name for dying—Going Home.

Campion P. Gavaler, O.S.B.